Radical social work in practice

Making a difference

Iain Ferguson and
Rona Woodward

BASW
BRITISH ASSOCIATION
OF SOCIAL WORKERS

First published in Great Britain in 2009 by

The Policy Press
University of Bristol
Fourth Floor
Beacon House
Queen's Road
Bristol BS8 1QU
UK

tel +44 (0)117 331 4054
fax +44 (0)117 331 4093
e-mail tpp-info@bristol.ac.uk
www.policypress.org.uk

North American office:
The Policy Press
c/o International Specialized Books Services (ISBS)
920 NE 58th Avenue, Suite 300
Portland, OR 97213-3786, USA
tel +1 503 287 3093 • fax +1 503 280 8832 • e-mail info@isbs.com

© The Policy Press 2009

British Library Cataloguing in Publication Data
A catalogue record for this book is available from the British Library.

Library of Congress Cataloging-in-Publication Data
A catalog record for this book has been requested.

ISBN 978 186134 991 0 paperback
ISBN 978 1 86134 992 7 hardcover

Cover design by The Policy Press.
Front cover: image kindly supplied by www.JohnBirdsall.co.uk
Printed and bound in Great Britain by the MPG Books Group.

SOCIAL WORK IN PRACTICE series P~P | BASW

Series editors: **Viviene Cree**, University of Edinburgh and
Steve Myers, University of Salford

"This series combines all the elements needed for a sound basis in 21st-century UK social work. Readers will gain a leading edge on the critical features of contemporary practice. It provides thoughtful and challenging reading for all, whether beginning students or experienced practitioners."
Jan Fook, Professor in Social Work Studies, University of Southampton

This important series sets new standards in introducing social workers to the ideas, values and knowledge base necessary for professional practice. Reflecting the current curricula of the new social work degree and post-qualifying programmes and structured around the National Occupational Standards, these core texts are designed for students undertaking professional training at all levels as well as fulfilling the needs of qualified staff seeking to update their skills or move into new areas of practice.

Editorial advisory board:
Suzy Braye, University of Sussex
Jim Campbell, Queen's University Belfast
Ravi Kohli, University of Bedfordshire
Jill Manthorpe, King's College London
Kate Morris, University of Birmingham
Lyn Nock, BASW
Joan Orme, University of Glasgow
Alison Shaw, The Policy Press

Other titles in the series:
Social work: Making a difference by Viviene Cree and Steve Myers

Social work and multi-agency working: Making a difference
edited by Kate Morris

Youth justice in practice: Making a difference by Bill Whyte

To the memory of Kate Cavanagh
(1951–2008): friend, colleague, feminist
and fighter for a social work profession
based on social justice

Contents

Preface

'All that is solid melts into air'

The British Prime Minister Harold Wilson once remarked that 'a week is a long time in politics'. The period between our agreement with The Policy Press to write this book and its eventual completion was, of course, considerably more than a week. Even then, however, we could not have begun to anticipate the extent to which the world we live in would have changed in that time. Then (that is, 18 months ago), neoliberalism, the ideology that says that allowing market forces free rein is the best way – indeed, the *only* way – to organise the global economy, reigned supreme. In this worldview, the real villain was the state. Against a post-war consensus that saw the state as having a positive role to play, both as an economic actor and in protecting its citizens from the worst ravages of capitalism, the new orthodoxy insisted that states were, at best, bit players in a globalised world, and, at worst, a burden and a drain on otherwise productive economies. For the neoliberal ideologues, however, both Conservative and New Labour, the state's real crime was in its response to the problems of poor people. In a complete reversal of the earlier consensus, the welfare state, once seen as the jewel in the crown of post-war British society, was now cast as the villain, due to its role in creating 'welfare dependency', by allegedly encouraging the poor in society – lone parents, unemployed people, disabled people and older people – to rely on state benefits.

In a very short space of time, all of this has changed, in Yeats' words, 'changed utterly'. In response to the worst global economic crisis since the 1930s, a crisis that has shattered the complacency of the world's governing classes and exposed as hubris the claim that neoliberal policies had ended forever the classic capitalist cycle of 'boom and bust', the state has been rediscovered as the saviour of the market. Now, with such transnational financial giants as AIG Insurance, the Royal Bank of Scotland and HBOS queuing up to accept financial help from their 'own' national states – help on a scale that far exceeds even their own wildest dreams – such dependency on the state no longer seems to be such a bad thing! All of the old assumptions have been thrown out of the window; in Marx's memorable phrase, 'all that is solid melts into air'.

What might this mean, then, for social work and for the people who rely on social work services? For us, it means two things. First, it is now clear that for many millions of people, especially the poorest sections of society, life is likely to become much worse over the next few years. With housing repossessions in the UK well up on previous years and, on some estimates, unemployment expected to rise to three million by the end of 2009, it seems likely that more children and families will find themselves living in poverty and that more people will experience mental health problems. Many of them will have little option in this situation but to look to the local social work department for help and assistance.

This brings us to our second point. The core argument of this book is that the currently dominant forms of social work are wholly inadequate to the task of providing help and support to the poorest, most oppressed, most vulnerable sections of society and that we need to look to the radical tradition to develop forms of practice that are genuinely capable of addressing people's material and emotional needs. Such forms of practice would prioritise the *relationship* between workers and service users while also being solidly rooted in values of social change and social justice. In our view, the economic turmoil we are currently experiencing strengthens the argument for such a new, radical social work. As we write, the newspapers are full of reports on the case of Baby 'P', the very young child who suffered abuse and eventual death at the hands of his carers. Against the predictable background of attempts to scapegoat those social workers involved, the realities of life in the local social work department are slowly emerging. The picture is not only one of inadequate resources, unrealistic caseloads and stressed-out staff but also one where social workers spend much more time sitting in front of computers, filling out bureaucratic forms, than they do in face-to-face contact with clients. In our view (and in the view of many who responded to a petition set up to challenge such scapegoating – www. socialworkfuture.org), it does not have to be like this. There *are* alternatives to what has been described as 'neoliberal social work'. Another social work is indeed possible. This book is a small contribution to the development of such a different form of social work practice.

Iain Ferguson and Rona Woodward
November 2008

Acknowledgements

Many people gave generously of their time to help us with this book. Our first vote of thanks must go to those who participated in the focus groups: the members of Stirling University's User and Carer Forum and our social work practice colleagues from the state and voluntary sectors. They all offered their time, their ideas and their experiences and their input was invaluable in shaping the way the book now looks. We are also grateful to the editorial staff at The Policy Press, who offered their support as need be and proved to be eternally patient with us. Finally, we would like to thank our friends who stayed interested and enthusiastic on our behalf and our families who put up with us throughout.

Social work in a divided society

> **Box 1.1: Cod's head soup**
>
> During the Depression of the 1930s, cookery classes were organised for women in poor communities in an attempt to help them to provide nutritious meals for their families despite their low incomes. One particular evening, a group of women were being taught how to make cod's head soup – a cheap and nourishing dish. At the end of the lesson the women were asked if they had any questions. 'Just one', said a member of the group, 'Whilst we're eating the cod's head soup, who's eating the cod?'. (Popay and Dhooge, 1989, p 140)

Introduction

The above anecdote first appeared in a collection of writings on radical social work in the late 1980s (Langan and Lee, 1989). In most respects, the 1930s' world of mass unemployment, soup kitchens and hunger marches to which it refers seems very far removed from the experience of social workers and social work students today. Yet as we move into the second decade of the 21st century, British society is once again shot through with massive levels of poverty and inequality. According to the writer Stuart Lansley, in his study *Rich Britain: The Rise and Rise of the New Super-Wealthy*: 'Britain has been slowly moving back in time – to levels of income inequality that prevailed more than half a century ago and to levels of wealth inequality of more than thirty years ago' (Lansley, 2006, p 29).

This sharp increase in inequality began under the Conservative governments of the 1980s and 1990s. It has, however, continued under New Labour since 1997. According to a report published in 2004 by the Office for National Statistics (ONS, 2004), the wealth of the super-rich doubled after Tony Blair came to power. Nearly 600,000 individuals in the top 1% of the UK wealth league owned assets worth £355 billion in 1996, the last full year of Conservative rule. By 2002 that had increased to £797 billion. Meanwhile, the wealth of the poorest 50% of the population shrank from

10% in 1986 towards the end of the Thatcher government's second term to 7% in 1996 and 5% in 2002. On average, each individual in the top 1% was £737,000 better off than just before Tony Blair arrived in Downing Street (ONS, 2004).

Levels of poverty also remain high. According to the most commonly used threshold of low income (60% or less of average household income), in 2005/06, around 13 million people were living in households below this low-income threshold – more than a fifth of the population. This number is less than it was in the early 1990s but much higher than it was in the early 1980s (www.poverty.org.uk). Child poverty, which fell during New Labour's second term of office, rose again by 100,000 in 2005/06 and one in three children is still living in poverty (www.savethechildren.org.uk).

However, even these figures may understate the extent of poverty and inequality in Britain today. For they were compiled at a time when the British economy was still being hailed as a major success story as a consequence of the market-driven, neoliberal policies pursued by both Conservative and New Labour governments since the early 1980s. Since 2007, however, a global economic crisis – which began in the US housing market, spread to the financial sector and was fuelled by spiralling food and fuel prices – has shown the hollowness of Britain's 'economic miracle' and exposed the limitations of market fundamentalist approaches (Elliot and Atkinson, 2008). For many millions of people, that crisis has had very immediate consequences. According to the website www.mysupermarket.co.uk, for example, a family that spent £100 a week on groceries in August 2007 one year on would be spending £127 – an additional £1,404 a year.

Social work, poverty and inequality

We live, then, in a divided society. That fact, and these figures, matter for social workers for one very simple reason: namely, that the overwhelming majority of people who use social work services in Britain today belong to that fifth of the population officially designated as 'poor' and, as such, are likely to be most affected by rising prices and economic insecurity. The observation of one American observer of the British social work scene in the early 1990s still holds true: '[T]he most striking characteristics that clients of social services have in common are poverty and deprivation. Often this is not mentioned … still, everyone in the business knows it' (Schorr, 1992, p 8).

The social work approach with which this book is concerned – radical social work – developed precisely out of a concern on the part of a significant minority of social workers in the late 1960s and early 1970s with the ways in which similar levels of poverty and inequality (recently 'rediscovered' by social policy researchers) were impacting on the lives of their clients and contributing to the problems that they were experiencing. These workers were also driven by a belief that social work could – and should – be about more than simply helping these clients to adjust to an unequal and oppressive society. Like many workers today, they believed that social workers' practice should make a positive difference to their clients' lives but also, often influenced by socialist ideas, that social workers had a role to play in creating a more socially just society.

The legacy of radical social work

In the next chapter, we shall explore the origins and ideas of the radical social work tradition in some detail. While never the dominant body of ideas, since their articulation in the 1970s radical analyses and perspectives have had a considerable impact on mainstream social work theory and practice. In Britain, for example, the argument that social workers should concern themselves with the structural roots of their clients' problems and should challenge the oppressions that they experience is one that will seem self-evident, 'common sense' even, to recent generations of social workers trained on texts such as Neil Thompson's (2006) *Anti-Discriminatory Practice*. At an international level, structural perspectives often underpin official statements and definitions of leading social work organisations, including the Code of Ethics of bodies such as the influential National Association of Social Workers in the US.

> ## Box 1.2: Social and political action
>
> Social workers should engage in social and political action that seeks to ensure that all people have equal access to the resources, employment, services and opportunities they require to meet their basic human needs and to develop fully. Social workers should ... advocate for changes in policy and legislation to improve social conditions in order to meet basic human needs and promote social justice ... with special regard for vulnerable, disadvantaged, oppressed and exploited groups.... [In this regard], social workers should act to prevent and eliminate domination of, exploitation of and discrimination against any person, group or class on the basis of race, ethnicity, national origin, sex, sexual orientation, age, marital status, political belief, religion, or mental or physical disability. (National Association of Social Workers, 1996, *Revised Code of Ethics*, cited in Reisch and Andrews, 2002, pp 1-2)

In truth, the gap between such radical rhetoric and the realities of social work practice is frequently huge. Even worse is the way in which radical language, including terms such as 'empowerment', which emerged from social movements against exploitation and oppression, is now frequently deployed in the service of a far from radical agenda of consumerism and privatisation (Langan, 2002). Nevertheless, neither the emergence of anti-discriminatory and anti-oppressive perspectives, nor the description of the social work role quoted earlier, would have been possible prior to the emergence of radical and structural perspectives in the 1970s and 1980s. The fact that such approaches and definitions are now part of the 'mainstream' gives some indication of the impact that these perspectives have had since that time.

The crisis of social work

The socialist-feminist writer Sheila Rowbotham wrote many years ago of how many women's struggles against oppression had, over the centuries, been 'hidden from history' (Rowbotham, 1975). Similarly, many social work students today are likely to be unaware either of the radical currents that developed in Britain, Canada and Australia during the 1970s or of other, even earlier, examples of radical practice and movements. Studying the experience of practitioners and activists from social work's past can provide both ideas and inspiration for social workers today. We shall return to that legacy of radical social work in the next chapter.

Our main interest in writing this book is not, however, to engage in historical research. Rather, it is to explore what radical approaches might mean in the very different world of 21st-century social work: the extent to which radical social work, in other words, can continue as a *living* tradition. Our starting point, like Bailey and Brake in the 1970s (Bailey and Brake, 1975), is a *critique* of existing social work. Here, we find ourselves in very good company. Even official publications such as *Changing Lives*, the 21st-Century Social Work Review in Scotland, commissioned by the (then) Scottish Executive, concluded that 'doing more of the same won't work' (Scottish Executive, 2006a, p 10). More generally, many social workers and social work academics would share the view expressed by Mark Lymbery in 2001 that 'social work in Britain is in a condition of crisis' (Lymbery, 2001, p 369). One indication of that discontent is that around 700 social work practitioners, academics and students have signed up to the Manifesto for Social Work and Social Justice, launched in 2004, which calls for a 'new, engaged practice' (Jones et al, 2004; www.liv.ac.uk/ssp/Social_Work_Manifesto.html). While there are, of course, different emphases in the analyses of factors contributing to the current crisis of social work, most would agree that the managerialist (or 'New Public Management') approaches, which have dominated social work for close to two decades and which have seen social work values come a very poor second to budgetary and financial considerations, have played a major role (Butler and Drakeford, 2001; Harris, 2003; Davis and Garrett, 2004; Hayes and Humphries, 2004b; Dustin, 2007; Price and Simpson, 2007).

Box 1.3: 'Social workers' skills are highly valued and increasingly relevant'

The International Federation of Social Work describes the mission of social work as being to 'enable all people to develop their full potential, enrich their lives and prevent dysfunction'. While we believe this is still valid to society today, we have found that in reality:

■ A culture of blame has developed in response to systemic failures to protect individuals and the wider community, which is forcing social workers into monitoring behaviour rather than actually helping people to make changes.

■ Heavy and inequitable caseloads often prevent social workers from tackling the complexities that lie behind the immediate need.

■ Demands exceed resources, resulting in social workers acting as gatekeepers, processing people through systems rather than working directly with individuals and families.

■ The constant pressure to deal with crises leaves little time for early intervention or for increasing the capacity of individuals, families and communities to find their own solutions.

'It is in this context that the 21st-Century Social Work Review in Scotland was commissioned to examine how social work services can adapt to meet present and future needs'.

Source: Scottish Executive (2006a, p 11)

Shrinking spaces

One effect of this managerialism has been to reduce considerably or even close down the 'spaces' in which even the most limited forms of progressive practice can take place. In Britain in the 1970s, the newly created generic social work teams led to a strengthened professional identity and were often seen as the places where workers could most easily organise and develop new forms of practice, both as professionals and as trade unionists. By the 1990s, however, the bureaucratisation of state social work was leading a significant minority to look to the voluntary sector as a place where they could practise 'real' social work, working closely with service users and carers. Now, however, as we show in Chapter Five, even those spaces are being closed off as voluntary sector organisations are increasingly expected to behave like businesses in a reinvented 'third sector'. Against that background, we agree with McDonald (2006) that mapping a way through this new world of managerialist, or neoliberal, social work makes it more important than ever for social workers to analyse and understand the contexts in which they work – organisational, economic and political. To help us to do that in this book, three chapters of the book are based on discussion with groups of state social workers (Chapter Four), voluntary sector social workers (Chapter Five) and service users and carers (Chapter Six). While the consumerist emphasis of New Labour policies has allowed some space for the voices of users and carers to be heard (even if often in a token way), the experience of frontline social workers over the past two decades has been almost completely ignored (with some notable exceptions: Jones, 2001, 2005; Cree and Davis, 2007). In a small way, these chapters seek to redress the balance.

'Resources of hope'

In common with other social work commentators, the authors of the Manifesto for Social Work and Social Justice referred to earlier began by noting that 'social work in Britain today has lost direction'. They went on to argue, however, that 'The starting point for this Manifesto … is that the "crisis of social work" can no longer be tolerated. We need to find more effective ways of resisting the dominant trends within social work and map ways forward for a new engaged practice' (Jones et al, 2004, cited in Lavalette and Ferguson, 2007, p 198).

As with other contemporary social movements, there is often much more agreement among participants about what they are against – in this case, the 'dominant trends within social work' – than what they are for. What, after all, would a 'new engaged practice' actually look like? And what are the 'resources of hope' that can help us create it?

Paradoxically, one of these resources may be the current level of dissatisfaction with social work in the UK and, above all, the feeling that 'it can't go on like this'. What is significant about this dissatisfaction is that it seems to extend well beyond the (small) number who would see themselves as 'radical' or even 'critical' social workers to include many 'traditional' social workers. A major source of frustration for many of those social workers interviewed for the Changing Lives report referred to earlier (Scottish Executive, 2006a), for example, was the lack of opportunity for relationship-based work with service users, one reason why many had entered the social work profession in the first place. At first sight, the notion that professional social work, wherever practised, could be anything other than relationship-based seems almost a contradiction in terms. Yet a key finding of Changing Lives was that many workers, particularly in local authority settings, felt that this aspect of their work had been 'eroded and devalued in recent years under the pressures of workloads, increased bureaucracy and a more mechanistic and technical approach to delivering services' (Scottish Executive, 2006a, p 28).

Since that lack of opportunity for direct work, along with trends towards the deprofessionalisation of social work and the dilution of social work values in both education and practice, stems directly from the neoliberal economic and social policies of all the main UK political parties, this suggests at least the possibility of developing, if not a movement, then at least a current or a network within social work based around a very different conception of what social work should be about (Ferguson, 2008, pp 130-6). In the final chapter of this book, we shall discuss some recent attempts to create such networks. Whether or not such a current or network should be seen as 'radical' or just 'real' social work, however, is a matter for discussion and debate. Chris Jones, for instance, having listed a number of examples of the ways in which social workers in the past have refused to collude with oppressive and stigmatising policies, argues that 'To my mind, we make a mistake to regard these kind of micro-practices as radical social work. For these practitioners this is the very nature of what social work should be and they are its guardians' (Jones, 2007, p 193).

In this respect at least, then, radical social work in the 21st century may be rather different from the 1970s' version and, in part, may at least reflect what many would recognise as 'just good social work', a suggestion to which we shall return in the final chapter.

Another 'resource of hope' is to be found in the social movements that have emerged in recent years. These are of two types. On the one hand, there are the movements of service users, including the disability movement and the mental health users' movement, which have already played such an important role in challenging both biomedical notions of disability and mental ill-health and the disabling services based on them. Alliances with these service user movements have to be at the heart of any new radical social work. On the other hand, there are the great global movements against neoliberalism and war that have appeared in the last decade and which have challenged the values and priorities of neoliberal globalisation. Again, if the business agenda in social work is to be effectively challenged, then building links with these broader movements of resistance and participating in their forums and debates is essential.

This book, then, is an attempt to explore and assess what a social work tradition, which we both see as profoundly valuable and relevant, might mean in the changed conditions of the 21st century. In that sense, it is an example of what Powell (2001, p 87) is referring to when he writes that 'Premature obituary notices have been written about radical social work. Its demise is unlikely. Radical social work is an authentic part of the social work tradition. It survives because it adapts and mutates.'

Who we are

We decided to write this book because, despite the current limitations of social work in the UK especially, we both remain convinced that social work is capable of playing a much greater role in the struggle for social justice than it does at present. That conviction is a product both of our individual politics and of our biographies, so we felt it might be useful to begin the book by saying who we are and how we arrived at these positions.

Rona writes: 'I was originally attracted to social work because, on the one hand, it seemed to provide opportunities to "make a difference" to the lives of people who were struggling and, on the other, it seemed a clear statement of political will. In the 1980s, as Thatcherism took hold in the UK, social work appeared to be one of the few, safe places remaining for someone committed to left-of-centre politics. I was raised in an active socialist family and studied sociology for my first degree. My interest in politics and social injustice is therefore a long-standing one. I completed my postgraduate degree in social work in 1990 and then worked in London and Edinburgh for 10 years, in both children and families and criminal justice services. It was during these years in frontline practice that the ambiguous nature of social work became particularly apparent to me. The "dual mandate" to both care for people and control their behaviour was additionally complicated for me because of social work's tendency to play down structural factors and to focus on individual and personal issues. It became increasingly difficult to "make a difference" as inequality grew throughout the 1980s and 1990s and notions of individual blame and shame took hold. Direct work with service users, however, reaffirmed for me over the years that my belief in humanity was not misplaced. At the same time, my direct work with student social workers, through practice teaching and lecturing, emphasised the extent to which students continued, on the whole, to see social work as a chance to right some wrongs.'

Iain writes: 'I began my life in social work in the mid-1970s as a community worker in Inverclyde, one of the most deprived areas of the West of Scotland. Community work fitted with my developing socialist beliefs. These stressed the possibility of collective action as a way both of changing social conditions and of increasing the confidence and political awareness of the people involved in that action. At the same time, I have always enjoyed working with individuals and families, particularly in relation to mental health issues, and, for that reason, decided to undertake professional social work education in 1980. Over the next 10 years, I worked in social work area teams in the Glasgow area, initially as a generic social worker, then as a lone-parent group worker, ending the decade as a community care social worker in a large psychiatric hospital. Entering social work education in the early 1990s gave me the opportunity to work with groups of service users in various action research and user-led projects and also to write and reflect on where social work is going. A frustration with the increasingly managerial direction of social work led me in 2004, with colleagues from Liverpool and Manchester, to write the Manifesto for Social Work and Social Justice, which has been the basis of a series of successful conferences in recent years. Despite its current loss of direction, I remain convinced that social work is still one of the few careers where it is possible to address both "public issues and private troubles" and that it continues to be (in the title of the conferences) "a profession worth fighting for".'

Overview of the book

As mentioned earlier, our main motivation for writing this book is neither historical nor nostalgic but rather to explore what radical social work perspectives might mean today. That said, we share the view that the experience of radical social workers in earlier decades is a rich resource for workers trying to develop more emancipatory forms of practice in the 21st century. Much of this history remains unknown to many social workers (and, we suspect, to many social work academics). Whether it be the role played by one of the founders of American social work, Jane Addams, in campaigning against world war in 1915; Clement Attlee's 1920 writings on 'the social worker as agitator' (Attlee, 1920, p 220); or the ideas of the magazine *Case Con*, which appeared from 1970 until 1977, there is much that contemporary social workers can learn from the struggles of those who went before. Chapter Two will seek to provide an overview of social work's radical history and considers what its legacy might be for social workers today.

Chapter Three will explore the contexts – political, economic, organisational – of social work practice in Britain today. Above all, this will involve documenting the ways in which social work has been reshaped by the neoliberal, market-based policies pursued by both Conservative and then New Labour governments over the last three decades.

Chapter Four, much of which is based on discussions with a group of local authority social workers, most of whom would be supportive of radical perspectives, will explore the possibilities for practising in an empowering way in the current situation, the constraints on such practice and the possibilities for challenging such constraints.

For growing numbers of social workers, especially during the 1990s, the voluntary sector seemed to offer a space in which more radical forms of practice, including campaigning work, advocacy work and service user involvement, still seemed possible. Chapter Five, built around a parallel discussion to that of Chapter Four, but this time involving social workers based in voluntary organisations, will discuss the extent to which the renamed 'third sector' continues to offer such possibilities.

One positive feature of the past decade has been the growth of service user organisation and influence within UK social work, albeit often within a very narrow, top-down framework of 'user involvement'. Advocates of radical social work in the 1970s argued for a very different, much more equal, relationship with their clients and we would similarly argue that any new radical social work has to be based on a coalition of workers, service users and carers. In the last of our three group discussions, Chapter Six will explore a group of service users' and carers' experiences of social work today, the kind of social work they would like to see and their views on user involvement.

Chapter Seven will look at collective approaches within social work. Like relationship-based work, such approaches have also been a victim of the dominance of individualist, care management frameworks over the past two decades. Yet, historically, they have been of considerable importance, especially within the radical tradition, and, in our view, need to be rediscovered. Here, three forms of collectivism in social work will be considered: community development approaches; social work and social movements; and forms of collective organisation among social workers themselves.

In the final chapter (Chapter Eight), we will seek to pull the threads of these arguments together to outline what we would see as being the key components of a new, radical social work for the 21st century. The past few years have seen the launch of a number of initiatives aimed at challenging the currently dominant forms of social work practice and we will consider how these might be built upon with a view to considerably strengthening social work's commitment to social justice.

Questions for discussion

➲ What experience, if any, have you had of poverty? In what ways does poverty affect people's quality of life and aspirations?

➲ Does it matter if inequality is growing in Britain, as long as the poor have their basic needs met?

➲ To what extent, if any, should social workers concern themselves with issues of poverty, oppression and social justice?

Suggested reading

➲ Davies, N. (1998) *Dark Heart: The Shocking Truth about Hidden Britain*, London: Vintage. A powerful and very readable exploration by a leading *Guardian* journalist of the nature and extent of poverty in Britain in the late 1990s and of the ways in which it destroys lives.

➲ Jones, C., Ferguson, I., Lavalette, M. and Penketh, L. (2004) *Social Work and Social Justice: A Manifesto for a New Engaged Practice*, Liverpool: University of Liverpool, www.liv.ac.uk/ ssp/Social_Work_Manifesto.html. An attempt by four British academics to explore the roots of the current crisis and point to some ways forward, which has formed the basis for a conference series and a loose national network (The Social Work Action Network).

➲ Scottish Executive (2006a) *Changing Lives: Report of the 21st Century Social Work Review*, Edinburgh: Scottish Executive. Semi-official response to the current state of social work in Scotland. Occasionally good on description of the problem but light on analysis and weak on prescriptions.

➲ There are also a number of very useful websites that provide up-to-date information on levels of poverty and inequality. Two of the best are www.poverty.org.uk and www.jrf.org.uk

The radical kernel

Box 2.1: Carol's story

When Miranda was still a baby, social work got her to a nursery every day. I had to go as well. They wanted to see how I acted with her. I had a nice flat, I did not starve her, they could not get me for neglect, so they made me attend to watch me. There is nothing worse than somebody else telling you what to do with your baby. You are constantly under their supervision. I had to go there, I could not relax. It was not a placement for Miranda to learn, it was a placement for me. They never saw me at home. I was still on tablets. They never provided the kind of day care which gave me a break. They never helped me get a fireguard. Did not see if I was cooking properly. I did not realize that I had a say in the matter. I took it for granted that because I was a single parent I had to do what they wanted. They never told me my rights. I had umpteen social workers. They did not help me to cope they just decided they would remove Miranda. I just wanted someone to talk to. (Holman, 1998, p 36)

Introduction

Carol's story comes from a collection of writings by people living in the Easterhouse area of Glasgow, edited by local community worker and former social work academic, Bob Holman (Holman, 1998). Easterhouse is one of several large housing projects (known in Scotland as 'schemes') built by Glasgow City Council in the 1950s to address post-war problems of poor housing in inner-city areas. Like similar housing projects across the UK, these schemes initially appeared to offer hope and a future to millions of people who until then had lived in overcrowded and unsanitary conditions. By the late 1960s, however, Easterhouse, like other schemes, had begun to experience a range of social problems, not the least of which was the emergence of a gang culture among its young men. A major reason for the problems in these areas was their lack of any infrastructure, such as shops, cinemas or community centres, as well as their geographical isolation from the city centre. The Scottish comedian, Billy Connolly, famously described the new Drumchapel scheme to which he moved as a child as 'a desert with windows'. These initial problems, however, were enormously compounded by the devastation caused by the social and economic policies of the Thatcher government of the 1980s, which led to mass unemployment and the development of a serious drug culture in many housing schemes.

Not surprisingly, such devastation throws up a range of social problems. No matter how resilient individuals or communities may be, when faced with such pressures their resources – social, emotional and financial – can become stretched, especially when they may have been very limited to begin with. In such situations, many, like Carol, will be forced to look beyond their own resources and networks and seek outside help. Alternatively, they may find such 'help' forced on them, often because of real concerns about the ways in which their behaviour may be causing risk or harm to other, more vulnerable, individuals. In either case, they may well find themselves in contact with social workers.

Beyond good intentions

While recent research suggests that many people *do* often find social work involvement helpful and supportive (Cree and Davis, 2007; Doel and Best, 2008), it is also the case that others, like Carol, by contrast experience such involvement as controlling and oppressive. There is a paradox here. In many years' experience as practitioners, practice teachers and tutors involved in student selection, both of us have found that most people who train to become social workers usually do so because they wish to 'make a difference', either in the sense of improving the lives of individuals who are experiencing difficulties or in the sense of contributing to the creation of a more just society, or both. It is rare, for example, to come across applicants to social work courses whose main goal is to remove children from the care of their parents or who have 'always wanted' to become a care manager. Their aspirations are generally somewhat higher and usually more altruistic. They have, in other words, good intentions. Yet as Carol's story suggests, such good intentions will not always guarantee anti-oppressive practice. No doubt on some occasions this will simply reflect the luck of the draw. As we will see in Chapter Six, some of the service users to whom we spoke in writing this book divided social workers into those who 'really cared' and 'were prepared to go the extra mile' and those who were 'only in it for the pay packet at the end of the month'. It would be strange indeed if in social work, as in every other profession, there were not some workers who were more caring, more competent and more committed than others. However, a central argument of this book – and of the radical social work tradition that it explores – is that the activities and good intentions of even the best social

workers, like the lives of those with whom they work, are often constrained
and distorted by the values and priorities of the society in which we live
– capitalism – as well as by the resources that they are allocated to do their
jobs. Even where workers want to work in anti-oppressive ways, as we
believe most do, it is often difficult for them to do so.

An ethical career

This is not to say, of course, that workers have *no* choices about how they
practise. Social work has rightly been described as an 'ethical career' (www.
peopleandplanet.org/ethicalcareers). This means that social workers need to
justify the decisions they make in their work with individuals, families and
communities by reference to the value base of the profession, now contained
in the Codes of Practice (GSCC, 2002). Whatever the structural constraints
they face, social workers who practise in an unethical manner, for example
by failing to show respect to their clients, by breaching confidentiality or
by behaving in a disempowering or abusive way towards service users, are
clearly failing to live up to the basic requirements of social work as an ethical
profession. The last thing that service users who experience oppression and
disrespect in every other area of their lives need is to encounter more of
the same when they seek help from social workers.

In addition, as the examples provided by Cree and Davis (2007) and Doel
and Best (2008) show, many people *do* value the help and support they
receive from social workers, often far more than the tabloid press would
have us believe. Moreover, as we shall see later in the chapter, Carol was
able to benefit from other forms of help, including the community social
work advocated and practised by Bob Holman over several decades. That
said, the 'spaces' for practising in an ethical and empowering manner have
been increasingly restricted by the managerial, budget-driven policies of
the last two decades, which we shall explore in the next three chapters. To
paraphrase Karl Marx, social workers work with service users but usually in
circumstances not of their own choosing. The impact of these constraints
– excessive caseloads, lack of supervision and support, unfilled vacancies
and a general lack of resources – is normally downplayed by politicians and
media hostile to social work, especially when a tragedy occurs such as the
death of a child in care. Then, the response is often a 'blaming' one, which
focuses on the shortcomings of the individual worker, abstracted from any
context whatsoever.

For us, this means that social work also has to be an ethical profession
in a second, more political, sense, mirrored in social work lecturer (and
later Labour Prime Minister) Clement Attlee's (1920) notion of 'the social
worker as agitator'. In Attlee's sense, good social work practice involves a

commitment not only to work in non-oppressive ways in direct work with service users but also to highlight and challenge policies and structural inequalities that undermine the health and well-being of those who use social work services. The recognition that 'empowerment' has to address wider issues of structural change as well as the way we work with individual service users is central to the radical tradition that we shall explore in this chapter.

Rediscovering the radical kernel

The American social work academic, James Midgley (2001), has observed that the radical (or, as he calls it, *activist*) tradition within social work, while historically one of the three main currents in international social work (the others being *remedial* and *developmental* approaches), has generally been the minority approach, the 'road not taken' in the title of a history of radical social work in the US (Reisch and Andrews, 2002). The reasons for this are not hard to see. Any approach that locates the sources of people's problems primarily in the structures of the society in which we live, and which encourages social workers to challenge these structures in their day-to-day practice, is likely to be viewed less favourably by governments and funding bodies than those approaches that instead highlight clients' individual inadequacies, faulty thought patterns or stunted emotional development. This has been especially true under the Conservative and New Labour governments of the last three decades, when not only radical approaches but also collective approaches in general, including community development, have fallen off the agenda of many social work courses and agencies. As this means that many students (and workers) will often be unaware of the 'radical kernel' in social work's past, this chapter will attempt to provide an overview of this tradition. First, we will look at social work's beginnings in the late 19th century and discuss the ways in which some practitioners and activists, both in Britain and in the US, sought to challenge the highly conservative ideas and practices of the leadership of the nascent profession and to develop alternative conceptions of helping. Second, we will fast-forward to Britain in the 1970s to consider the emergence of that model of practice that consciously proclaimed itself as 'radical social work'. Third, we will consider what radical social work might mean today. Finally, we will return briefly to the example of Carol and consider what help she found useful and why.

The early politics of social work

Mainstream social workers and social work academics have often tended to shy away from approaches that they see as too 'political'. Yet as Powell (2001, p 27) has observed, politics have shaped social work since its infancy. The dominant politics of early social work, however, as reflected in the leadership of the Charity Organisation Society (COS), were far from radical. By and large they tended to mirror the concerns, fears and prejudices of the Victorian middle and upper classes. In one way or another, these fears and concerns related to the 'problem of the poor', which was seen as threatening the political and social fabric of London and other British cities (Mooney, 1998). There were several aspects to this 'problem'. First, there was concern over the widening social and geographical gulf between the wealthy middle classes who inhabited the West End on the one hand and 'Outcast London', the teeming and impoverished masses to the East, on the other (Stedman Jones, 1984). Vast wealth flourished a mere stone's throw away from the areas of indescribable poverty in which the casual poor lived, yet there was little or no contact between members of these different social classes. As well as the fear of crime, there was also a growing concern that with the disappearance of the traditional hierarchical relationships and habits of deference that had characterised feudal society, this rising class of unskilled, uneducated workers could pose a real political threat to the existing social order. As one prominent commentator wrote in the *Contemporary Review* in 1885:

> I am deeply convinced that the time is approaching when this seething mass of humanity will shake the social fabric, unless we grapple with it more earnestly than we have done…. The proletariat may strangle us unless we teach it the same virtues which have elevated the other classes of society. (Samuel Smith, cited in Charlton, 2000, p 55)

This fear was not without foundation. Middle-class society had already been shaken by bread riots and violent demonstrations in the late 1860s, while the mid-1880s were to witness the development of a near revolutionary situation in the capital, followed soon after by a huge strike wave involving the casual poor (Stedman Jones, 1984, pp 281ff). These events fuelled another fear of the wealthier classes, namely the spread of socialist ideas.

Unsurprisingly, the dominant explanations for the spread of poverty and the unrest to which it gave rise did not implicate either laissez-faire capitalism or the operation of the 1834 Poor Law (with its dreaded workhouse provision for those deemed unwilling or unable to work) in the emergence of the 'problem of the poor'. Rather, in a punitive discourse, which was to enjoy a remarkable revival in the form of 'underclass' theory more than a century later, the problem was seen as the product of three main factors. First, there was misguided interference with market forces, for example in the form of proposals for state aid to the poor, including old age pensions and free school meals. Such proposals, it was argued, were not only economically wrong-headed but also undermined family responsibility. Second, there was the perceived negative impact of charity. As a result of the middle-class fears described earlier, there had been a huge growth in the number of charities set up to relieve poverty and in the amount of money they dispersed. Such 'indiscriminate alms giving' was seen as undermining character and family responsibility, in very much the same way as the welfare state has often been portrayed in more recent times as 'part of the problem' rather than 'part of the solution', since it allegedly fosters 'welfare dependency'. No less importantly, however, such indiscriminate charity was seen as wasteful since it made no distinction between those capable of benefiting from such help (the 'deserving poor') and those on whom it was wasted (the 'undeserving poor'). Underpinning this distinction was a social Darwinism (based on the theory known as *eugenics*) that some people were beyond redemption as a result of their genetic or 'constitutional' inheritance and should therefore be abandoned to the workhouse (or worse).

These ideas, widespread within the Victorian middle and upper classes, also underpinned the theory and practice of the earliest British social work organisation, the Charity Organisation Society (COS), founded in 1869. Thus, the charity was vehemently opposed to the introduction of old age pensions and free school meals; it perceived indiscriminate charity as the greatest evil facing the casual poor of the East End and its leading members were sometimes prepared to countenance the most extreme solutions for those regarded as beyond help. An example of the latter is usefully captured in a letter from one Ella Pycroft to the social reformer Beatrice Webb, at that time active in COS but later to become its most prominent critic:

> Do you remember telling me when I first met you how you had helped to bring about the death of an opium eater in Soho? I couldn't understand then how you could have done such a thing but now I have come to think that you were right, and right in a most large-minded, far-seeing way. I am coming to see more and more that it is useless to help the helpless, that the truly kind thing is to let the weak go to the wall, and get out of the strong people's way as fast as possible. (cited in Harrison, 2000, p 108)

As Webb's biographer comments on this letter, 'Depriving the undeserving poor of life was only a logical extension of depriving them of their liberties, and it was even more economical' (Harrison, 2000, p 108). The method of casework, the detailed investigation of an individual's circumstances and character, which was later to become the core social work approach, was developed by COS leaders precisely to enable visitors and full-time workers to distinguish between the 'deserving' and 'undeserving' poor.

COS's 'friendly' critics

In the course of the 1880s, criticisms of COS began to grow. These came from two main sources: from within COS itself, sometimes from those who had played a leading role in its development, and from activists in the emerging socialist and labour movements. The criticisms of this second group will be considered in the next section with those that came from within COS discussed here.

Friendly critics included individuals like Maude Royden, a volunteer in the 1890s with the Liverpool Central Relief Society. The Liverpool Society shared many of the same ideas as the London-based COS. Despite coming from a wealthy background, Royden seems to have struggled with the philosophy and practice of COS. She hated, for example, the class superiority that underpinned its 'friendly visiting' and wrote to a friend that 'I shouldn't be grateful if Lady Warwick, e.g., came to see me every week, to get me to put a few shillings into a provident fund … I should be mad' (cited in Pedersen, 2004, p 86). She found it unsurprising that the young, working-class women found the club activities of games and singing organised by COS boring and stated that, given the choice, she too 'would prefer to loaf in the streets with a (presumably) attractive young man' (cited in Pedersen, 2004, p 86). Finally, the constant injunction against any act that would lead to 'demoralisation' baffled her and, in exasperation, she wrote:

> I can think of nothing but the dangers of 'giving'. They appear to me so great as to be almost paralysing. You mustn't give money; or clothes. If you help them to get work, wouldn't it be better for their independence or character if they got it themselves? It seems to me that the only people worth helping are the ones who don't need it. (cited in Pedersen, 2004, p 86)

In his study of COS, Jones argues that one important reason for the introduction of professional social work education at the turn of the 19th century was to combat the effects of such 'contamination' of these new social workers by their clients, which suggests that Royden was far from being the only person to think in this way (Jones, 1983). More significant, however, were the critiques of individuals such as Canon Barnett, founder of the Toynbee Hall Settlement in the East End of London, and Sydney and Beatrice Webb, leading members of the Fabian Society and central to the formation of the British Labour Party.

The Settlement movement, of which Toynbee Hall was the first example (although it was quickly followed by others in London and other British cities), is usually seen as the second major source of contemporary social work in both Britain and the US. Like COS, its aim was to promote social harmony through active citizenship, an aim that was to be achieved by persuading the educated middle-class young from universities to spend a period of time living and working among the poor, assisting them through education and example, and promoting social reform on their behalf (Powell, 2001, pp 38-40). It was initiated by Barnett in the wake of the rise of mass unemployment in the early 1880s and reflected his growing conviction that state aid, rather than the 'scientific philanthropy' practised by COS, was necessary to eliminate poverty.

Some commentators have seen in the Settlement movement the origins of the progressive or radical tradition within social work. Powell, for example, suggests that opposition to COS's social Darwinism was at the root of the split between COS and the Settlement movement that took place in 1885, and that essentially 'this was a clash between positivism and humanism, between those who advocated science and those who promoted social reform as an appropriate response to poverty' (Powell, 2001, p 34). Similarly, the Canadian social work writer, Bob Mullaly (1997, p 24), suggests that the focus of the Settlements was 'to reform society rather than the person. Out of this heritage came another of social work's primary methods of intervention, a self-help model of community organisation that focused on participation of the poor, community development and social action.'

There are certainly similarities between the methods adopted by Settlements, such as Toynbee Hall, and the community development and community social work approaches of the 1960s and 1970s (Chapter Seven). Moreover, in the US especially, the Settlement movement did indeed develop in a radical direction, and in the period before the First World War was actively involved in organising trade unions, supporting strikes and campaigning around social issues such as child labour and factory conditions (Reisch and Andrews, 2002). According to one commentator, 'social workers, regarded by politicians and businessmen as misguided zealots, came to be recognized as the most effective reformers of their generation' (Morrison, cited in Powell, 2001, p 39). The British movement, however, seems to have been less radical. In his study of 'outcast London', for example, Stedman Jones (1984) suggests that a key concern of thinkers like Canon Barnett, faced with the spread of radical socialist ideas and growing social unrest, was to incorporate the more 'respectable' sections of the working class into discussions around social reform. As he notes, however, the 'counterpart of wooing the respectable working class, in this new form of liberalism, was the espousal of a more coercive and interventionist policy towards the "residuum"' (1984, p 303). Thus, Barnett's 'practicable socialism' allowed for the establishment of compulsory labour colonies for the casual poor as a solution to the problem of unemployment, and he argued that 'It is a shocking thing to say of men created in God's image, but it is true that the extinction of the unemployed would add to the wealth of the country.... The existence of the unemployed is a fact and the fact constitutes a danger to the wealth and well-being of the community' (Stedman Jones, 1984, p 303).

Contemporary critics from the neoliberal think tank *Civitas* have also argued that Barnett's differences with COS have been greatly exaggerated and concerned issues of methods rather than goals (Whelan, 2001, p 58). While then, like the Fabian thinkers Sydney and Beatrice Webb, his experience of COS led him to the view that philanthropy alone would not solve the 'problem' of the poor and that state intervention was required, as the earlier quote suggests, there were very definite limits to his humanism.

'Hidden from history': political agitation and social work

If the radicalism of Canon Barnett and the Webbs was of a rather timid variety, the same cannot be said of the social work activities of some of their contemporaries. As one of us has argued elsewhere (Ferguson and Lavalette, 2007b), there is a rich tradition of more radical forms of helping that has been largely written out of the history of social work. Reference was made earlier, for example, to Clement Attlee's notion of the 'social worker as agitator'. In his biography, in a chapter entitled 'Social work and politics', he gives examples of what that meant in practice. Between 1909 and 1914, he was involved in organising soup kitchens for the families of striking dockers, campaigning against the Poor Law, and organising free school meals. Similarly, individuals like Emmeline Pethick-Lawrence, Sylvia Pankhurst and George Lansbury made little distinction between their political activities as socialists and suffragists and their efforts to provide direct support to the poor. Pethick-Lawrence, for example, began life as a voluntary social worker with the London Methodist Mission in 1891. Shocked by the poverty that she encountered, she helped set up a cooperative dressmaking business to help young women escape the exploitation and long hours of the East End tailoring trades. Like the American Settlements, but in marked contrast to later British social workers, she was concerned not only with people's home lives but also with their conditions in the workplace. Like COS, she saw the importance of gathering information about her clients' lives but of a rather different type: 'It became our business to study the industrial question as it affected the girls' employment, the hours, the wages, and the conditions' (cited in Ferguson and Lavalette, 2007b, p 17).

These more challenging notions of the social work task were marginalised, however, by the trend towards professionalisation in the years before the Second World War, as well as by the increasingly widely held view that growing state intervention made any form of social work irrelevant and obsolete. The result, according to Jones, is that:

> Despite many changes in the language and knowledge base since the end of the nineteenth century, social work has remained an activity that is not only class specific, but also has continued to practise as if the primary cause of clients' problems are located in their behaviour, morality and deficient family relationships. (Jones, 2002a, p 44)

Exploring what he calls the 'critical impulses' in social work remains important, however, both as a reminder to us that things could have turned out differently and also as a resource in the construction of a different type of social work in our own time. As he notes, by far the most significant of these critical impulses emerged in the 1970s and it is to a consideration of the radical ideas and practices that flourished in that period that we now turn.

Radical social work in the 1970s

Several factors contributed to the emergence of a distinct radical social work tradition in the UK in the 1970s. First, there was the 'rediscovery of poverty'. The combination of economic boom and the growth of the welfare state in the post-war period meant that many working-class people did experience real improvements in their standard of living during these years. However, as studies in the 1960s by poverty researchers like Peter Townsend and influential television plays like Ken Loach's *Cathy Come Home* demonstrated, issues of poverty, poor housing and homelessness continued to dominate the lives of many people, and frequently brought them into contact with social workers. Against that background, the limitations of the psychosocial approaches then common within mainstream social work were becoming increasingly apparent. Their inability to address the material and structural problems that clients faced was graphically highlighted by studies such as *The Client Speaks* (Mayer and Timms, 1970) (subtitled *Working-Class Impressions of Casework*). As well as providing some examples of good practice, Mayer and Timms' book also contains painful accounts of working-class clients emerging dazed and confused from contact with social workers who were inclined to locate their clients' current difficulties in paying bills and managing their finances in their problematic early relationships with their parents. The limitations of such approaches were cruelly, if accurately, parodied in a cartoon that appeared in the magazine *Case Con*, where an earnest young social worker is shown interviewing a clearly poor and demoralised young mother living in a slum house and asking her 'But tell me, Mrs Jones, how do you *feel* about your rats?'.

This critique of a form of individual casework that was seen as blaming clients for what were essentially structural problems, coupled with the promotion of other approaches, which to a greater extent did address these issues, including community work and welfare rights strategies, was an important element of the emerging more radical approach. This aspect of radical social work was subsequently criticised by some for contributing to a devaluing of what they saw as the more progressive aspects of psychoanalytic approaches and, more generally, for leading to an underestimation of the potential for radicalism inherent in individual work with service users (Fook, 1993). While many supporters of radical approaches did see little value in the casework approaches then prevalent, that hostility is perhaps understandable, given its often pathologising nature. Significantly, however, Bailey and Brake, in what is usually seen as the seminal text of the movement, were at pains to emphasise that they did not reject casework per se but only its more oppressive variants (Bailey and Brake, 1975, p 9).

A second factor contributing to the emergence of radical social work was the rapid growth in trade unionism among social workers during the 1970s. That growth was a product of two factors. First, there were the major legislative and organisational changes that redefined the role and status of social work at the end of the 1960s. In an attempt to overcome the fragmentation and overspecialisation of existing social work services, the Kilbrandon Report in Scotland (1964) and the Seebohm Report in England and Wales (1968) had recommended the creation of a unified social work profession, based in area teams that offered a generic service. These large, new area teams (described by one writer as 'Seebohm factories'; Simpkin, 1983) helped create a new collective identity among social workers and an awareness of themselves as local government *workers* who shared common interests with other workers in the authority. On the one hand, this led to a rapid rise in the numbers joining the local government trade union NALGO (later to become part of UNISON). On the other, it undermined elitist notions of professionalism, not only in relation to other workers but also in relation to people using social work services, who were increasingly seen as sharing common class interests with social workers. The critique of professionalism, then, was a second key plank of this emerging approach.

A third factor contributing to a new collective consciousness among social workers was the huge wave of popular protest that swept through not only Britain but also most of the world at the end of the 1960s. This was a period where, in the words of one writer, 'There occurred a spontaneous combustion of rebellious spirits around the world', a time when 'people were rebelling over disparate issues, and had in common only that desire to rebel, ideas about how to do it, a sense of alienation from the established order, and a profound distaste for authoritarianism in any form' (Kurlansky, 2004, p xvii).

The seminal year of that rebellion was 1968, with its high point being the 'May events' in Paris, student protests that sparked off a General Strike involving 10 million French workers. What was important about 1968, however, was that it saw the emergence of a *global* movement, with participants in one country identifying with the struggles of those in another. Thus, for example, the courage and determination of civil rights protestors challenging racism in the American South provided the inspiration for the oppressed Catholic minority in Northern Ireland to form their own civil rights organisations and challenge the sectarianism of the 'Orange State'. Similarly, the struggle of black people against racism led women, gay people and other oppressed minorities to question their place in society (as well as in the social movements of the time), leading to the formation of the women's liberation movement, the Gay Liberation Front and so on. The names by which these movements chose to be known drew directly from the most crucial struggle of these years, namely the struggle of the Vietnamese people, under the leadership of the National Liberation Front, against the American occupation of their country (Neale, 2001).

Humm (1992, p 1) describes feminism as a 'social force', which recognises that 'women are less valued than men' but argues that 'women can consciously and collectively change their social place'. As a 'social force', feminism has had some influence on the development of social work at various points in its history (Dominelli, 2002a), in recognition of the fact that most service users and carers were (and still are) women, as were (and still are) most social workers (Hanmer and Statham, 1988; White, 2006). The first wave of feminism in modern, industrialised societies (approximately the 1790s to the 1920s) sought to establish rights for women, and encourage their participation in social and political circles (Sanders, 2001). An almost 50-year lull in feminist thought and action followed, however (a lull that some would call a 'counter-offensive'; Thornham, 2001, p 29), before the second wave of feminism emerged (the 1960s to the 1980s). Second-wave feminism not only reintroduced the idea that the social conditions of women needed to improve but also proposed a more radical restructuring by demanding that, once and for all, women should be freed from patriarchal repression and subordination (Humm, 1992; Thornham, 2001). While acknowledging that there is no single feminism – socialist, Marxist, lesbian, liberal and radical ideas all feature in second-wave feminism (Humm, 1992) – feminists agree that women experience subordination and, therefore, require liberation (Abbott and Wallace, 1997).

All of these movements impacted on social work theory and practice in several different ways. At the most general level, they gave rise to a questioning of many of the 'taken-for-granted', common-sense assumptions that underpinned the dominant ideology of the post-war period. Feminism, for example, challenged dominant ideas about the role of women in society and the superiority of the nuclear family (Langan, 1992). Similarly, the gay rights movement disputed the 'deviant' nature of homosexuality (Cretney, 2006), while the mental health users' movement redefined the nature of mental illness and professional power (Crossley, 1999). Since these ideas and institutions were also central to much social work practice, inevitably the role of social workers in promoting and reinforcing such ideas came under scrutiny. That questioning was particularly acute, moreover, within the universities, which were undergoing a period of massive expansion, especially in the rapidly growing discipline of sociology. For example, both Marxist ideas and radical deviancy theories, which explored the ways in which particular individuals and groups were labelled as deviant or problematic, struck a chord with many students. At the same time, feminist ideas, while never fully hitting the mainstream of social work education or practice (McNay, 1992), began to influence a significant number of women and men in social work (White, 2006). As a student social worker in 1989, one of us (Rona) joined with several of her student colleagues (men and women) to request that gender issues and feminist approaches be covered in more depth within her particular postgraduate course. It is important, therefore, to emphasise that the women's movement 'resulted in a systematic critique of social work at many levels'; feminism highlighted 'the gender-blindness which has characterised social work policy and literature' (Cree and Cavanagh, 1996, pp 1-2). Finally, as Pearson has noted, for many sociology graduates, a job in social work, with all its limitations, appeared to offer a way of earning a living while also hanging on to their ideals and dreams of social change (Pearson, 1975).

Ideas and strategies

Box 2.2: No easy answers

Every day of the week, every week of the year, social workers (including probation officers, educational social workers, hospital social workers, community workers and local authority social workers) see the utter failure of social work to meet the real needs of the people it purports to help. Faced with this failure, some social workers despair and leave to do other jobs, some hide behind the facade of professionalism and scramble up the social work ladder regardless and some grit their teeth and just get on with the job, remaining helplessly aware of the dismal reality. Of course, some do not see anything wrong in the first place.

Case Con is an organisation of social workers (in the broadest sense) attempting to give an answer to the contradictions that we face. It offers no magic solutions, no way in which you can go to work tomorrow and practise some miraculous new form of social work that does meet the needs of your 'clients'. It would be nice if there were such an easy answer, but we believe that the problems and frustrations we face daily are inextricably linked to the society we live in, and that we can only understand what needs to be done if we understand how the welfare state, of which social services are a part, has developed, and what pressures it is subject to. It is the purpose of this manifesto to trace briefly this development, to see how it affects us and our relationships to the rest of society, and above all to start working out what we can do about it. (Introduction to the *Case Con Manifesto*, in Bailey and Brake, 1975, p 144)

What, then, were the ideas and forms of practice that made up radical social work in this period? As Powell (2001) shows in his sympathetic account of the movement, a number of different political currents and radical ideas contributed to this new movement. It contained activists, for example, who were revolutionary socialists (mainly grouped around the magazine *Case Con* – see Box 2.2), others who were drawn to the Communist Party and the Left of the Labour Party (Corrigan and Leonard, 1978) and also many non-aligned social workers who were influenced by the generally radical milieu of the time. That milieu was informed by the ideas of the radical educationalist, Ivan Illich, the American-based German philosopher, Herbert Marcuse, the Brazilian educationalist, Paulo Freire, and – particularly important in the area of mental health social work – the British 'anti-psychiatrist', R.D. Laing. Radical social work, then, is best seen as a broad movement, the diverse strands of which are well represented in Bailey and Brake's (1975) edited collection. Whatever their differences, moreover, as Powell (2001) observes, most of those involved were united around two broad objectives: first, the transformation of social work through closer involvement with the struggles of collective social movements, such as the newly emerging claimants' unions or the longer-established tenants' associations; and second, the critique of traditional social work practice. Powell (2001, p 86) cites Cloward and Piven's 1990 indictment of traditional casework practice:

> We have to break with the professional doctrine that ascribes virtually all of the problems that clients experience to defects in personality development and family relationships. It must be understood that this doctrine is as much a political ideology as an explanation of human behaviour. It is an ideology that directs clients to blame themselves for their travails rather than the economic and social institutions that produce many of them.

How then did this new movement influence social work theory and practice? It did so in three main ways. First, in terms of social work education, group work and community work approaches became a feature of some courses (although by no means all), as did welfare benefits teaching and an increased emphasis on sociological approaches. Second, in terms of practice, collective approaches, including group work, as well as community work, approaches, became more widespread. Strathclyde Social Work Department, for example, the largest in the UK, invested heavily in employing community workers (Barr, 1991). While it is true that work with individuals continued to constitute the major part of most workers' caseloads, a significant minority sought to incorporate community work activities within their workloads.

Third, and most importantly, radical social work transformed the profession's value base. During the 1980s and the 1990s, it became common among critics of radical social work (and some disillusioned former radicals) to assert that while there had been plenty of radical theory around in the 1970s, there was less evidence of radical *practice*. Certainly, the constraints of working in local authority social work departments placed limits on the scope for translating radical aspirations into reality (although this should not be exaggerated: where workers made the case for a community work approach, there were possibilities even within statutory social work teams). During this period, for example, one of the authors (Iain) negotiated time to work with a local housing action group while working as a generic social worker in an inner-city area of Glasgow). There were, however, as the *Case Con Manifesto* acknowledged, 'no easy answers'. The real shift, though, was in the areas of values and the ways in which clients were perceived. Bailey and Brake (1975, p 9) themselves had argued that 'Radical social work, we feel, is essentially understanding the position of the oppressed in the context of the social and economic structure they live in'. There is considerable evidence that, by the end of the 1980s, this perspective had become the 'common sense' of much of the profession. Thus, an influential edited collection published in 1989 noted the shift that was taking place from 'traditional social work' values to 'anti-oppressive values' (Shardlow, 1989), a move reflected, for example, in the emphasis placed on anti-racist practice within the new Diploma in Social Work.

Radical social work: the legacy

Like many of the other social movements that developed in the 1960s and 1970s, radical social work experienced a decline in the 1980s. The main reason for this is not hard to see. Both in Britain and internationally, newly elected right-wing governments (principally the Conservatives under Margaret Thatcher in Britain and Ronald Reagan's Republican administration in the US) sought to recoup their losses, both economic and ideological, of the previous two decades by attacking those whom they perceived as responsible for them (Harvey, 2005). While the principal target of this attack in Britain was the trade union movement, the rise of the 'New Right' also affected social workers. This was less because of any threat they posed to British capitalism than because they were seen as providing a useful scapegoat. More than any other profession, social workers were seen as 'soft' on precisely those groups – unemployed people, lone parents, young offenders – whom the Conservatives and their media allies wished to brand as 'scroungers' and 'the underclass'. In the face of these attacks (which were to re-emerge in the 1990s, as part of the crusade against 'political correctness') the social work profession became increasingly defensive and sought to play down its radicalism.

Anti-oppressive practice and critical social work

Despite these attacks, however, radical ideas did survive, although in a rather different form. In the UK, for example, the late 1980s saw the growing influence of anti-racist social work, feminist social work and anti-oppressive practice, while, in Australia and Canada, 'critical' (or 'structural') social work became the generic term for what were often very similar approaches. Dominelli (2002), one of the leading exponents of anti-oppressive practice in the UK, has defined it as:

> a form of social work practice which addresses social divisions and structural inequalities in the work that is done with 'clients' (users) or workers. Anti-oppressive practice aims to provide more appropriate and sensitive services by responding to people's needs regardless of their social status. Anti-oppressive practice embodies a person-centred philosophy, an egalitarian value system concerned with reducing the deleterious effects of structural inequalities upon people's lives; a methodology focusing on both process and outcome; and a way of structuring relationships between individuals that aims to empower users by reducing the negative effects of hierarchy in

their immediate interaction and the work they do together. (cited in Adams et al, 2002, p 6)

Despite a hostile political climate, anti-oppressive perspectives made some progress in the late 1980s and early 1990s, figuring prominently, for example, in the Diploma in Social Work, the new professional social work qualification introduced in the UK at that time. The fact that students were now required to explore the ways in which different forms of structural oppression, notably sexism, racism and disablism, shaped the lives of people who used social work services was a step forward. It made it less likely, for example, that students – or workers – would now operate on the basis of such 'common-sense' assumptions as 'Asian families look after their own old people' and more likely that they would begin to question, for example, the gender-based nature of much 'informal care'. Nor was this increased awareness of the influence of structural oppression in people's lives confined to issues of gender and class. The emergence in the 1980s and 1990s of (often extremely militant) collective organisations of disabled people, people with mental health problems and other marginalised groups meant that social models of disability and mental health also became more prominent within social work education, challenging biomedical approaches that located people's difficulties in their biology. (The development of 'user involvement' in services, which also began at this time, will be explored in Chapter Six.)

Anti-oppressive perspectives, therefore, have been important in heightening awareness of the multiple oppressions experienced by service users in a way that earlier versions of radical social work sometimes failed to do. However they are not without their limitations, two of which will be noted here. First, the 1980s saw a shift within critical social theory away from analyses of oppression as rooted in the structures of capitalism to a focus instead on 'identity' and 'difference' (Williams, 1996). Detached from social and economic structures, within postmodern approaches in particular, oppression becomes something that is increasingly seen as subjectively defined, while capital, the state and oppressive social structures disappear. Not surprisingly, the main victim of this approach has been class, which as 'classism' (Thompson, 2006) becomes, at best, just one more form of oppression, no more or less important than, say, middle-class angst. Yet as we saw in Chapter One, class and poverty continue to be the main factors shaping the lives of millions of people, including most social work clients.

Second, in contrast to 1970s' radical social work, the emphasis of anti-oppressive practice has often tended to be on changing the attitudes, behaviour and language of individual workers, as opposed to changing the conditions in which clients live (with the emphasis on language in particular making it an easy target for the accusation of 'political correctness'). On the one hand, this meant that anti-oppressive practice, especially as a requirement within the Diploma in Social Work (now replaced by a new, degree-level professional qualification), was often experienced by students and tutors alike as involving a top-down moralism, seemingly more concerned with ensuring the correct behaviours and attitudes on the part of students than with real social change. As one critic of the Central Council for Education and Training in Social Work (CCETSW), which oversaw these changes, commented at the time:

> Judgement, censure, righteousness and watchfulness – all of which must perforce attend anti-sexism and anti-racism if they are to succeed – are also the defining attributes of the ideal-typical puritan. To the puritan falls the heavy obligation of practising extreme strictness in matters of morals and a developed sensitivity to breaches in the correct code of behaviour or thought. (cited in Langan, 2002, p 216; see also Penketh, 2001)

Some of these strengths and weaknesses are also present in the 'critical social work' literature that has emerged over the past two decades principally in Australia (Allan et al, 2003) and in Canada (where it is sometimes referred to as 'structural social work'; Mullaly, 1997). As Healy (2005, p 173) notes, in its broadest sense, critical social work embraces a very wide range of oppositional perspectives, including Marxism, feminism and anti-oppressive approaches. Adherents of critical social work in this broad sense have produced an impressive body of work, which includes, among other things, incisive analyses of the ways in which managerialism has reshaped the context of social work practice (McDonald, 2006), as well as powerful critiques of the treatment of asylum seekers in Australia and elsewhere, which fit perfectly with Attlee's description of the 'social worker as agitator' (Fraser and Briskman, 2004; Briskman et al, 2008). In its narrower sense, however, 'critical social work' refers to the acceptance within much of this literature of post-structuralist and postmodern perspectives (see, for example, Leonard, 1997; Pease and Fook, 1999a). As critics of these perspectives have noted (Davis and Garrett, 2004), in practice they tend to lead away from the kind of structural analysis that needs to underpin genuinely radical approaches and, in their celebration of individualism and localism, sometimes seem only very indirectly concerned with wider themes of social justice and social change (for a longer discussion, see Ferguson, 2008, Chapter 7).

Conclusion: Carol's story

We will end this chapter, as we began it, with Carol's story from Bob Holman's (1998) volume, since it embodies many of the themes we have been outlining in this chapter. First, Carol's account of her life and the difficulties she faced shows the impossibility of trying to make sense of any individual's feelings, thoughts and actions without seeing them in the wider context of their past and current situation – in Carol's case, her experience of disability, gender oppression and poverty on the one hand, and resilience and resistance on the other. Second, the story might never have been produced had not one of the most inspiring and committed exponents of the radical tradition (albeit that Bob Holman might not describe himself in quite these terms) seen the importance of giving local people a voice, even if – or, rather, especially because – that voice gives a very different picture of social work than more official versions. Finally, Carol's story is important because, as it progresses, it shows that 'help' and 'caring' do not have to be oppressive, controlling and paternalistic. With Holman's support, Carol became involved in a variety of local organisations, including a food cooperative and a local breast-feeding initiative. In her words:

> Over the years, it has helped me to help others. I like helping people.... Later I was elected chairperson. It gave me a purpose. The volunteers were mainly elderly people, so some were like mother figures or granny figures to me. They respected me and it gave me more confidence. (Holman, 1998, p 45)

Reflecting on her involvement in this and other community activities she notes:

> I am a different person now from 10 years ago. I look at things in their wholeness now instead of jumping in. I used to be constantly negative, now I am more positive. It is because I met people who supported me. I have been helped by going to the Sally [Salvation Army], by being a part of the food co-op and by the Breast feeding Initiative. (Holman, 1998, pp 47–8)

Carol's experience suggests that different, non-oppressive forms of helping *are* possible, based on factors such as giving people a valued role, treating them with respect and building their confidence. In the next two chapters we shall explore the extent to which it is possible for social workers to practise in such empowering ways in the often very non-empowering context of statutory social work in the 21st century.

Questions for discussion

⮑   What similarities can you identify between the attitudes and values of the 19th-century Charity Organisation Society and current government attitudes towards 'welfare dependency'?

⮑   Can social work ever be 'non-political'?

⮑   In your experience, what are the main barriers facing social workers today who wish to pursue a more radical approach? How might these be overcome?

Suggestions for further reading

⮑   Bailey, R. and Brake, M. (eds) (1975) *Radical Social Work*, London: Edward Arnold. The founding text of radical social work in Britain – more than 30 years old but still well worth reading. Contains the *Case Con Manifesto*.

⮑   Hayes, D. and Humphries, B. (eds) (2004) *Social Work, Immigration and Asylum: Debates, Dilemmas and Ethical Issues for Social Work and Social Care*, London: Jessica Kingsley Publishers. The current treatment of asylum seekers in Britain and elsewhere poses a major challenge to social work values. These writers have been in the forefront of those arguing for a much more vigorous response.

⮑   Lavalette, M. and Ferguson, I. (eds) (2007) *International Social Work and the Radical Tradition*, London: Venture Press. Challenges the notion that radical social work is an exclusively British phenomenon by bringing together examples of radical practice from nine countries, including Palestine, Slovenia and South Africa.

⮑   Price, V. and Simpson, G. (2007) *Transforming Society? Social Work and Sociology*, Bristol: The Policy Press. A recent text that reasserts the value of the 'sociological imagination' for social workers and argues for the adoption of a more structural approach.

Neoliberalism and social work

Box 3.1: Aileen

On qualifying as a social worker three years ago, Aileen, a 28-year-old, white woman, worked in a busy children's services team in a large Scottish city. Although much of her time was spent at the 'heavy end' of social work – child protection and looked-after children – she received regular, high-quality supervision and had the benefit of working alongside experienced and dedicated colleagues. She found the work demanding but stimulating, having opportunities to develop her knowledge and skills through training courses and sufficient time and support to work directly with children and families. She learned much about structural discrimination and the vagaries of political life from her colleagues and from the service users with whom she worked. As a result, she became more critical in terms of her own understanding of society and of social work's place within it, a criticality that translated into her commitment to anti-oppressive approaches to practice.

Six months ago, when Aileen's partner secured a job in a different part of Scotland, Aileen moved too, accepting a post in another local authority children's services team. This experience is a very different one, however. While the needs of children and their families remain ever complex, and their experiences of exclusion and stigma become ever more apparent, Aileen finds little space either to work directly with service users or to improve her professional skills. Assessments are procedural and time-limited; supervision is focused on targets and outcomes; most 'intervention' is provided by voluntary sector agencies; many colleagues seem stressed out and wedded to their computers; and there is a palpable tension between frontline staff and senior management. In her new team, social work seems to Aileen like 'two dirty words'. She is, however, committed to local authority social work and, at this stage in her career, is not prepared to 'walk away from the job'.

Introduction

The previous chapter emphasised the extent to which social work remains, at least in principle, committed to practice that makes a positive difference to the lives of people in need; practice that is concerned both with individual well-being and with wider issues of social justice. While radicalism might well have been 'the road not taken', radical ideas influenced social work in the direction of ethical, value-based practice. Perhaps this is illustrated most plainly in the current, and widely accepted, definition of what social work should be (IFSW/IASSW, 2000, www.ifsw.org/en/f38000138.html):

> The social work profession promotes social change, problem solving in human relationships and the empowerment and liberation of people to enhance well-being. Utilising theories of human behaviour and social systems, social work intervenes at points where people interact with their environments. Principles of human rights and social justice are fundamental to social work.

The previous chapter, however, also highlighted how difficult it is now for social workers to find sufficient space to practise in anti-oppressive ways. Indeed, the experiences of Aileen, as outlined in Box 3.1, illustrate just how far removed some social work services have become both from the needs and rights of service users and from the motivations and commitments of their own frontline practitioners. Aileen's current circumstances may look fairly bleak but her story gives us some hope too. It emphasises that different social work organisations work in different ways and that practising social work does not have to be a grim experience. We can see that one social work agency – Aileen's first employer – provided her with room to practise creatively and critically while offering users supportive, often empowering, services, albeit within the confines of statutory control. This, of course, prompts the question as to why Aileen's current employer is determined to do the opposite.

In Chapter Four we seek to explore the constraints and possibilities within the state social work sector in a bid to explain why workers' and service users' experiences are so variable. Beforehand, this chapter provides a wider economic, social and political analysis of the problems and tensions that now beset the social work profession, and of the increasingly complex personal and social needs that now blight the lives of so many service users. In particular, we consider the development of neoliberalism in recent years. We discuss the significance of neoliberal policies for social work, with emphasis on marketisation and managerialism, increasing poverty and inequality and discourses of demonisation and stigmatisation. This focus on neoliberalism is essential because of its destructive effects on British institutions, communities and individuals.

While many social work service users and carers face increasing poverty, inequality and marginalisation, social workers now struggle more than ever to retain their commitment to working with the 'social', as well as the 'individual'. In this chapter, we argue that social work in the UK has borne the brunt of efforts by both Conservative and New Labour politicians to marginalise the role of the state in dealing with social problems and to introduce a business agenda to welfare services. We do not suggest that the UK stands alone – the forces of managerialism and marketisation have had a detrimental effect across the Western world, South America, Africa and beyond (McDonald, 2006; Ferguson and Lavalette, 2007a). It is our contention, however, that UK social work is particularly at risk: it has lost much of its focus on holistic approaches; it has misplaced its commitment to social justice, despite official rhetoric to the contrary; it has bought into punitive notions of individual responsibility, which sit uncomfortably with concepts of partnership and empowerment; and it has embraced, uncritically on the whole, the managerial agenda.

The tone of this chapter is inevitably subdued – we struggle to put any kind of positive spin on neoliberalism and its effects. We will, however, end by revisiting Aileen's story because, while she may be discontent, she is not without hope and energy. In demonstrating the ways in which Aileen, alongside some of her colleagues, begins to think about how to put the 'social' back into social work, we will both end this chapter optimistically, and pave the way for the next chapter, which explores not just the constraints of working within the state social work sector but also the possibilities.

The neoliberal discourse

> The neoliberal discourse is not a discourse like others ... it is a 'strong discourse' which is so strong and so hard to fight because it has behind it all the powers of a world of power relations. (Bourdieu, 1998, p 95)

By the time the Labour government of Clement Atlee introduced the welfare state to the UK in 1945, plans were firmly in place for a wide-ranging programme of social legislation in a bid to tackle poverty, unemployment and inequality. In the years of optimism that followed the Second World War, there was cross-party consensus that the state had some responsibility to support and protect its citizens. This broad agreement in relation to social welfare was echoed in the US for a time – the New Deal of the 1930s and the War on Poverty of the 1960s – despite a traditional reliance on private markets (Gilbert and Tang, 1995). It was seen also in many parts of Europe, until the market began to assume a much greater global importance in the provision of health and welfare from the early 1970s onwards (Johnson, 1995a).

The Western economic boom of the 1950s and 1960s, based on high employment, low inflation and improved standards of living, began to unravel in the late 1960s, giving rise to a crisis in capitalism among Western countries (Harvey, 2005; Glyn, 2006). By the early 1970s, many Western domestic economies were in fiscal chaos, with rising unemployment and inflation. Seeing catastrophe looming, big business reacted strongly against what it understood to be a dangerous drain on its profits. Bowing to business pressure, the Labour government – in power in the UK between 1974 and 1979 – responded by introducing monetarist measures, designed both to protect business and to reduce its own spending deficits (Glyn, 2006). Pure capitalism, now based on powerful monetarist and increasingly neoliberal forces, began to reassert itself as the dominant economic ideology.

Neoliberalism may be a relatively new set of economic and social policies but it is now so dominant within richer economies that it would appear to have taken on 'the status of business as usual' (Glyn, 2006, p vii). Neoliberalism is now fully established: 'Low inflation, quiescent industrial relations, freedom for capital to chase profitable opportunities without restraint and the domination of market-based solutions have become familiar features of the economic landscape' (Glyn, 2006, p vii).

Globalisation

The term 'globalisation' is potentially a problematic one. Although there is little doubt that global interconnectedness is growing (Cochrane and Pain, 2004), and 'hardly anyone would say that globalization is not altering the rules of the political "game"' (Rapley, 2004, p 5), the existence of several related trends and processes make it difficult to define. Before we turn to a discussion of the neoliberal agenda, and a consideration of its effects, we need to be clear that it is argued by some (Rosenberg, 2000; Webb, 2003; Kelly and Prokhovnik, 2004) that the existence of pervasive and harmful global forces is at best overemphasised and at worst fallacious. Our starting point, however, is that globalisation is very real in that the internationalisation of economics has become a powerful force; it has become increasingly 'difficult to speak out against the world power of the world market' (Beck, 2000, p 9). At the same time, globalisation can be seen as a 'neoliberal fable' put across powerfully to justify the 'need' to reduce public spending and maximise individual and company profit (Bourdieu, 1998). Indeed, the accumulation of capital has been the 'fundamental driving force of the economy' (Glyn,

2006, p 86) for centuries and rich countries have often looked to exploit world markets to strengthen their wealth and power base.

It is beyond the scope of this book to debate, in full, globalisation and either radical or sceptical responses to it. We will summarise our stance as follows, however: although globalisation is far from sounding the death knell for individual nation states (Rapley, 2004), the neoliberally informed, global marketplace, with its unrivalled ability to accumulate capital for employers and investors (Bourdieu, 1998), has come to dominate in relatively recent times, producing 'fabulous riches' for some and 'terrible poverty' for others (Beck, 2000, p 33). While neoliberal globalisation may be associated with capital's unending search for accumulation, we consider that its presiding over growing inequality is neither inevitable nor natural.

1979-97: Conservatism, Thatcherism and the New Right in the UK

The neoliberal revolution is closely associated with both Margaret Thatcher in the UK and Ronald Reagan in the US from 1979 onwards (Harvey, 2005).[1] This is not to suggest that Thatcher and Reagan were the first proponents of neoliberalism – 'Thatcherism was not invented by Mrs Thatcher' (Bourdieu, 1998, p 30) – because recent neoliberal doctrine is inextricably linked with the work of both early liberal economists (Adam Smith and Jeremy Bentham, among others) and later 20th-century exponents of a free market (for example, Hayek, 1949, 1960; Friedman, 1962 [1982]). Indeed, as mentioned above, despite manifesto claims to the contrary, welfare cuts began in the mid-1970s in the UK under a Wilson–Callaghan Labour government caught between a profit squeeze, militant labour and the power of the Bank of England (Callinicos, 2001). There was never any real intention on the part of Labour governments of the 1960s and 1970s to challenge the power of the business elite: 'Harold Wilson's honours list looked like the pay–off for financial contributions' (Lansley, 2006, p 156).

Margaret Thatcher's Conservative government was swept to power in 1979 in the UK with a clear message about where the Conservative Party stood in relation to public services. For Thatcher, the welfare state was 'the corrupt brake on progress' (Rapley, 2004, p 79) and had created a 'culture of dependency that undermined independence and sapped entrepreneurialism, thereby restricting economic growth and damaging competitiveness' (Miller, 2004, p 24).

Strange as it may seem, radical critics sometimes highlighted similar concerns to those of their New Right counterparts in their recognition of the need for restructuring of public services and the weakening of professional power. The solutions proposed by both camps, however, were markedly different (Miller, 2004). Where radicals promoted the development of community initiatives, and greater powers for trade unions and user movements, the 'political operation' engineered by Margaret Thatcher and her New Right libertarians advocated the introduction of free market, private enterprise to break up the state's near monopoly on welfare provision and promote 'individual rationality' (Bourdieu, 1998, p 95). For Thatcher and Reagan there was 'no alternative' (Harvey, 2005) to laissez-faire marketisation; individualism and entrepreneurialism were to be freed from years of state control.

Neoliberal marketisation underpinned a number of fundamental shifts in UK values, culture, policy and, ultimately, social life. Underpinning the process was the assumption that wealth 'trickles down' and that the poor will somehow benefit as the rich become richer. This licence for the rich to print money, to become the new 'super-rich' (Lansley, 2006), seemingly placed the UK and the US, at least for a time, among the most successful economies but with the poorest records on equality and quality of life (UNICEF, 2007).

At the same time, the erosion of the welfare state and the privatisation of public services began (Jones and Novak, 1993; Miller, 2004). Non-state forms of welfare – first the family but thereafter communities, self-help groups and private and independent agencies – emerged and there was an expansion in semi-professional and professional jobs at the expense of skilled and unskilled work. There was also an increase in part-time, contractual and insecure work, especially for women (Pantazis and Ruspini, 2006). In short, blatant money-making for some was accompanied both by a deliberate squeeze on the benefits and opportunities available to the UK's poorest people and the calculated introduction of a business agenda to the public sector. On the basis of erroneous claims about efficiency and effectiveness, public sector language was transformed, markets created and a new layer of generic managers introduced. Increasingly, terms like 'value for money' and 'consumers' were bandied about as managerial principles and practices took hold.

The early legacy of the New Right: fractured lives

The preferentiality towards the rich and powerful associated with the introduction of the first neoliberal economic and social policies in the UK was seen most powerfully in the rate at which the gap between rich and poor increased and inequality grew. Between 1979 and 1994, real incomes of those in the poorest 10th of the population fell by 13% while the average income rose by 40% and the income of the richest rose by 63% (Oppenheim, 1997). Gordon (2000) translates these percentages into actual sums of money to demonstrate that the poorest 10% in the UK was £520 a year worse off by the time 18 years of Conservative government came to an end in 1997, yet the richest 10% was even richer, to the sum of £12,220 each year. As will be seen later, this trend has continued under New Labour, despite progress being made in relation to some children and adults (JRF, 2006).

Free market libertarianism, and the unfettered generation of wealth, was, however, only one aspect of the New Right agenda of Margaret Thatcher's Conservative government. It also consisted of neoconservative, moral traditionalism and concern about a perceived growth in permissiveness. Therefore, as well as supporting the marketisation of modern welfare provision, the New Right advocated a return to core British values and social morality (Beck, 2000), a call that quickly entered the political mainstream in the 1980s and early 1990s. John Major, Thatcher's Conservative successor, following the in-party coup that ousted her as Prime Minister in 1990, introduced what he called his 'back to basics' campaign in 1993. Major adopted a highly moral tone in his pursuance of family values and, despite the extent to which scandal stalked the House of Commons at the time – a number of Conservative politicians were found in all sorts of economic, political and sexual compromises (Sergeant, 1998) – the political focus remained on the behaviour of the 'feckless' and 'undeserving' poor. What emerged as a result were powerful notions of a 'putative underclass' (MacDonald and Marsh, 2005, p 6), a concept that owes much to the writings of Charles Murray (1990, 1994).

For New Right supporters like Murray, the underclass consists of 'another kind of poor' (Murray, 1990, p 17), the unemployed and the welfare dependent, located there due to their own individual failings and a generous welfare state. For more critical commentators (Powell, 2001; MacDonald and Marsh, 2005), however, the underclass – not that this potentially stigmatising term is a favoured one – is differentiated from the majority population because it is excluded on the basis of age, gender and ethnicity, as well as employment status. It therefore includes not only lone parents, disabled people, older people, working-class young people and people from minority ethnic backgrounds but also those excluded because of additional, often moralistic, prejudices: travelling people, people suffering from HIV/AIDS, drug users, refugees and asylum seekers (Preston, 2005). Margaret Thatcher and the Conservative government seemed perfectly comfortable with the fact that, by the end of their years in power, there existed a number of people and communities adrift from the rest of society, demonised, stigmatised and marginalised (Davies, 1998).

The New Right assault on public services: 'it's social work but not as we know it!'

By 1997, social services in the UK had changed beyond recognition in both the statutory and voluntary sectors. This was due, in part, to the increasing inequality and greater social need discussed earlier, which exacerbated the problems faced by already poor and deprived people, some of whom were in contact with social services. At the same time, though, the free market and its emphasis on private sector values and structures began to promote both privatisation and profiteering in public services (Johnson, 1995b). Conservative governments of the 1980s and early 1990s introduced the contracting out of public services (compulsory competitive tendering), privatised aspects of health and social care provision (private health insurance and hospitals and private residential care for older people) and ushered in a range of new charges in the public sector (council house rents increased and the cost of prescriptions, eye care and dental services soared).

Within social work itself, new legal arrangements for community care (the 1990 NHS and Community Care Act) introduced practice based on care management principles, while presiding over deinstitutionalisation (primarily for older people and those with disabilities) (Lymbery, 2004). Residential care homes and long-stay hospitals emptied and social services departments became increasingly involved in assessing the needs of those earmarked for care in the community, but they did so under a new model, one based on a split between the purchaser and the provider. Social workers were now required to assess wide-ranging personal and social needs but not necessarily to provide the services to meet these needs. This shift paved the way for further privatisation of traditional social work roles and services as social workers in the state sector became increasingly required to 'buy in' services from private or independent agencies (Johnson, 1995b). As local authority social workers (especially those working in adult services) became more concerned with assessing need, planning care, arranging contracts and purchasing services, so their role became more administration and less direct work with service users. Sturges (1996, cited in Lymbery, 2004, p 162) suggests that early care management directives in social work led ultimately to routinised and standardised working practices, larger workloads, deskilling of the workforce and a retreat from the traditional emphasis on care and counselling. All of this took place in a climate of tight budgetary control, leaving social workers with an apparently impossible task, 'to reconcile the inadequacy of resources with apparently infinite demand' (Lymbery, 2004, p 163). Given the extent to which financial motivations underpinned moves towards community care in the UK (Johnson, 1995b), why would anything else have been expected from a government committed to profit and privatisation?

1997 to the present day: New Labour, modernisation and the 'Third Way'

In 1997, the Labour Party came to power after 18 years of Conservative government with then Prime Minister, Tony Blair, at the helm. Although Labour politicians stressed their commitment to addressing poverty and inequality, they also stated their desire to continue with the modernisation of public services and to distance themselves from 'old' Labour socialism – hence the rebranding as 'New Labour' and the pursuance of a 'Third Way', distinct both from the New Right (neoliberalism) and 'old' Labour (social democracy). 'Old' Labour had spent 18 years on the parliamentary opposition benches while neoliberalism and neoconservatism took root in the UK. The view taken by the more powerful people within the Labour Party was that any continued truck with socialism would not appeal to the new middle and upper classes – more likely to vote than their working-class counterparts – and that a new direction was needed if the election was to be won. Tony Blair who, with a few key advisers, spearheaded this shift within the Labour Party and the landslide Labour victory in the General Election of 1997, was clear from the outset that Thatcher and company had made much of Britain 'great' again. As a result, although the Conservative government of John Major had gone down in a sea of sleaze and corruption, and many people in the UK were desperate for change, economic and social policy was not earmarked for major reconstruction under New Labour.

The stated goal of the Third Way is to adapt old-style social democracy to meet the demands of a new world (Giddens, 1998). Hence, 'public services need to modernise in order to compete within global free market capitalism' (Miller, 2004, p 35). In relation to public services, several core policies emerged during the first few years of the Blair premiership in the UK, which served to develop and strengthen the marketisation and early managerialism introduced by the Conservatives (Jordan with Jordan, 2001). Despite declaring its support for state provision, New Labour quickly rediscovered the mixed economy of welfare, pointing to the need for a plurality of service providers to respond to increasingly complex social and personal problems.[2] In a mixed economy of welfare, while multiple providers could, in theory, offer a more diverse range of services, there is always the risk of 'privatisation by the back door' (Miller, 2004, p 51) and further marginalisation of the state. For New Labour, the argument has always been that it is the end result in service provision that matters, not how or by whom the service is delivered (Drakeford, 2006). How realistic is it, though, for market-sector organisations to provide services to potentially troublesome 'involuntary clients'? Surely it is too much of a financial risk to chase after those who do not want support or who have particularly challenging behaviour or problems? As Miller (2004) suggests, the 'heavy end' of provision in a mixed economy of welfare is likely to be left to the state and, at times, the voluntary sector while the 'for-profit' sector takes its pick of the rewarding or profitable work.

In keeping with its Conservative predecessors, New Labour saw fit to strengthen business language and practices within the public sector. Third Way welfare reform and modernisation is, for New Labour, a process requiring the increased involvement of business people, groups and institutions in the management and delivery of public services (Farnsworth, 2006). A commitment to managerial reform, based on notions of 'what works' and 'best value', and driven by the discipline of the 'three Es' – economy, efficiency and effectiveness – was at the heart of New Labour's programme. As Harris (2003, p 43) argues, the previous Conservative governments and their New Labour successors share one key assumption – that capitalist enterprise is good: 'more economical, efficient and effective than the public sector in providing services'. The rise of 'managerialism' appears to be demoralising and stressing social workers in equal measure, however, by devaluing their professional role, and challenging their values and principles, especially those who work in the state sector (Lymbery, 2001).

Managerialism

> Managerialism is a set of beliefs and practices that assumes better management will resolve a wide range of economic and social problems.... Managerialism itself is a reflection of the powerful dominance of market capitalism. (Tsui and Cheung, 2004, pp 437-8)

Managerialism refers to 'the inroads made by management into professional autonomy and power' (Adams, 2002, p 250) or, to put it less politely, 'a culture of "never mind the quality, feel the width"' (Ferguson et al, 2002, p 86). While government and professional ideology has embraced concepts of empowerment and participation in respect of social work service users (Jordan, 2001), managerialist forces are often experienced as alienating and disempowering by social workers; again the 'solution' then becomes part of the 'problem'. If care management, introduced by the previous Conservative government in the UK, heralded the beginning of a new phase of managerialism in public services, New Labour's version of managerialism has seen it become a powerful ideological stance within state welfare organisations.

Box 3.2: Managerialism in action

Taking social work to illustrate the process, we can see just how sophisticated managerial practices have become:

- There are 'top-down', centralised processes of financial control and evaluation.
- Policy makers and managers define and control the nature of the professional task with bureaucratic procedures (guidelines, assessment frameworks and checklists, performance targets) and quantification of output to discipline 'slow workers' and improve quality standards.
- Practitioners struggle to exercise professional judgement and discretion, based on their own knowledge, skills and practice wisdom.
- Social workers are no longer professionals but instead are employees who assess the services required by service users, decide how and by whom these services will be provided and ensure that services meet value-for-money criteria.
- There is an emphasis on 'cash and contracts' rather than 'care and concern' (Tsui and Cheung, 2004, p 440) – while practitioners face an increasingly insecure, stressful and demoralised working environment, service users experience social work services as reactive rather than preventive, delivered in a climate of budget cuts and resource shortages, despite growing social need.

See Jordan (2001); Powell (2001); Harris (2003); Lymbery (2004); Tsui and Cheung (2004); Banks (2006); White and Harris (2007).

When New Labour Prime Minister, Tony Blair, stood down in June 2007, and was replaced by Gordon Brown, it did not take long for a political announcement to be made that seemed to herald a new era of trust in public services. Top-down targets were to be scrapped and local authorities and health trusts were to be left alone to set their own priorities (Carvel, 2007). Whether this move improves the situation in which social workers, especially those employed in the state sector, find themselves will require a 'wait and see' approach. We can be forgiven for not holding out much hope here, however. As argued previously, neither New nor 'old' Labour offered much to temper the market economy and it would seem that the restructuring of health, education, legal and welfare systems is continuing at full tilt under Gordon Brown's premiership. In the run-up to local council elections in England in 2008, New Labour, although still describing itself as a social democratic party, continued on its contradictory path. For example, the party emphasised not only its desire to strengthen communities but also its wish to develop its approach to anti-social behaviour and to tackle the immigration and asylum 'problem'. In addition, the party, while praising 'hard-working' families and claiming to have lifted 600,000 children out of poverty, stressed that new tests are needed to ensure that 'benefit cheats' are not falsely receiving Incapacity Benefit and added significant costs to the tax burden of poorer, single people. As we write, the global economy is being threatened by a credit crunch yet public money is going to bail out large banking companies rather than support individuals struggling to pay soaring housing, food and fuel costs.

Poverty and inequality

While supporters of the Third Way deny that it is simply neoliberalism with a different name (Giddens, 2000), we suggest the opposite; that it has taken neoliberal doctrine and policies and, in the words of Alex Callinicos (2001, p 121), 'radicalized them'. Arguably, the global bequest of the new, social democratic policies of the 1990s and 2000s is similar to the legacy of the New Right of the 1970s and 1980s: increased capital accumulation and privatisation alongside growing inequality of income and opportunity, social marginalisation and moral authoritarianism. A report published by UNICEF (2007) emphasises that the UK now compares very poorly with its rich counterparts in terms of the proportion of children whose lives are blighted by poverty, by inequality – in terms of access to education and health opportunities – and by unacceptable levels of risk and fear.

The New Labour government of Tony Blair stressed its desire to reduce unemployment (Flaherty et al, 2004) primarily because it is associated in its collective mind with poverty and social exclusion, both of which it aims to tackle at some level in a bid to soften the harsher side of neoliberalism. New Labour, therefore, introduced a series of 'New Deal', 'work first' programmes for young people, lone parents, people over the age of 50, disabled people and those who are 'long-term unemployed' (Flaherty et al, 2004). That some individuals are moving into employment is evident, but many people are simply working for their benefits on 'workfare' principles (Ferguson et al, 2002) and what real work there is tends to be part time, low paid and insecure, which does little to tackle poverty (Flaherty et al, 2004; Preston, 2005; JRF, 2006). New Labour continues, however, with its emphasis on work as the way out of poverty. In March 2007, then Secretary of State for Work and Pensions, John Hutton, admitted that, despite a range of anti-poverty initiatives and some progress having been made, the number of children living in relative poverty in England and Wales had risen by

100,000 between 2004/05 and 2005/06, while the number of children living in absolute poverty remained unchanged in the period (DWP, 2007a). The answer to this, rather than decisive universal policies likely to tackle barriers to social inclusion and mobility, was another 'New Deal', this time for families. Although New Labour recognised that lifting children and families out of poverty requires strong policy initiatives in relation to tax, benefits, health, housing and education, no particular measures were identified and parental employment remained a central element of the reform programme (DWP, 2007b).

A report on poverty in Scotland (JRF, 2006) suggested that the Scottish Executive, unlike its London counterpart, had met UK targets for reducing child poverty – official rates fell by one quarter since 1998/99. This is not to suggest that poverty in Scotland is no longer a cause for concern. The Child Poverty Action Group is clear (McKendrick et al, 2007) that Scottish policy also needs to develop in much more creative, redistributive ways if poverty is to be tackled. Poverty, however, is only one side of the coin. Inequality continues to grow across the UK and, indeed, is at a 40-year high (JRF, 2007). New Labour's acceptance of growing inequality fails to take account of powerful research evidence suggesting that it is inequality, not poverty in itself, that makes societies sick, sad and dysfunctional; it is the stress of being at the bottom of the heap – low of status, disrespected and lacking control over one's destiny – that leads to reduced life expectancy (Wilkinson, 2005). The apparent failure of successive governments to seriously tackle income inequality, and to only tinker with core and breadline poverty (JRF, 2007), leaves some of the UK's most vulnerable children and their families continuing to inhabit a 'quite different world' from the rest of society (Jones, 2002b, p 118). The implications for social work of this political indifference (indifference at best – calculation may be more apt) towards particular individuals and groups within UK society are clear: 'This means that the degree of poverty endured by people in receipt of social services has increased, thereby exacerbating a range of other social problems' (Lymbery, 2001, p 373).

Demonisation and stigmatisation: getting tough

Box 3.3: Practice example

Damon is 16 years old and lives with his mother, brother and sister on a peripheral housing scheme in a Scottish city. His mother has mental health problems, struggles with heroin addiction and has financial difficulties, owing large sums of money to home shopping catalogues. Damon and his siblings have been in local authority care several times in the past but all three children

▶

are now at home. Damon has not attended a mainstream school since he was 11 and has problems both reading and writing. In addition, he uses alcohol and cannabis recreationally. Since his return to his mother's care, three months ago, Damon tends to hang around his neighbourhood, often with other young men around his age. He has no income of his own but sometimes he can 'borrow' money from his mother to buy alcohol and drugs. At other times he steals alcohol from the nearest supermarket. Neighbours have become increasingly distressed by what they see as Damon's anti-social behaviour. They allege that he is foul-mouthed and aggressive and that it is he who is the main source of the vandalism that now makes the local shopping centre such an unpleasant place to visit.

Social workers and the police are frequent visitors to the family but believe that the advice they offer goes 'unheeded'. The local authority housing department has now applied for an Anti-Social Behaviour Order in respect of Damon. At the same time, the social work department is considering a Parenting Order in respect of his mother, who feels that she has little control over Damon and admits that she continues to struggle with the care of her youngest children. It is now time, as far as the local authority and police are concerned, to 'get real' about the likelihood of supporting this family to change. Tougher measures are needed!

Discussion

Assuming that Damon's neighbours are correct in their assessment of him, few would argue that his behaviour is acceptable and many would expect 'something to be done'. There is, however, no quick fix. Damon and his family are well known to the police and social workers. Over the years, different workers will have tried different approaches, some of which will have helped the family to cope while others will simply have added to the family's feelings of injustice, alienation and despair. The social work job in Damon's situation will never be an easy one: where do we start when individuals and families are so overwhelmed by multiple social and personal problems? Complex needs require creative responses based on strong relationships between workers and service users, a willingness on the part of professionals to stay the course and a readiness to listen to families and to help them seek their own solutions (Jordan, 2007). The anti-social behaviour and the parenting order may satisfy neighbours' desire for action but just how likely is it that these potentially punitive and stigmatising methods will overturn years of social, emotional and economic deprivation?

Within a mixed economy of welfare, the state is usually assumed to be being 'rolled back' in terms of publicly funded provision (but see Harman, 2008) but, at the same time, New Labour has substantially extended the power of the state in certain areas. With its focus on particular individuals, families and groups – those already excluded from mainstream society – legislation in relation to asylum and anti-social behaviour is of particular relevance for social work. In 2006, New Labour introduced legislation – the Immigration, Nationality and Asylum Act – which includes provision to limit individuals' right of appeal, to deprive individuals of British citizenship (when doing so is deemed 'conducive to the public good') and to strengthen border controls. When accompanied by the 2006 Terrorism Act, which creates new terrorist offences (apparently in response to New Labour's sense of an unprecedented terrorist threat now looming in the UK), it may not be going too far to suggest that immigration and asylum is increasingly associated not just with potential danger but also with terrorism. If so, the likelihood is that an already stigmatised, 'second-class' group of people living in the UK will be marginalised all the more, whether through distrust of their motives, denial of access to services or, ultimately, criminalisation and punishment.

The UK-wide Crime and Disorder Act was introduced in 1998 and was followed by more specific anti-social behaviour legislation in England (2003) and Scotland (2004). The message behind the introduction of such legislation is that the family is expected to play the key role in socialising and moralising individual members of society (Ferguson et al, 2002) and that, where certain families fail to behave in a way that is acceptable to wider society, the state must act; this is what we saw happening in Damon's situation in Box 3.3. That families are placed at the centre of Third Way politics in this way leaves plenty of room for families equally to be demonised when things go wrong. As Muncie and Goldson (2006) argue, the Parenting Orders that were introduced with this new raft of anti-social behaviour legislation pay little heed to the extent of social deprivation in the UK but rather focus on the personal failings of particular families. As a result, already dislocated parents and their children – the state is rarely interested in the parental 'failings' of those who earn hundreds of thousands of pounds each year while leaving their children to the care of nannies and private school educators – become targets of a new risk-based agenda, which emphasises responsibilities rather than personal or social needs (Walters and Woodward, 2007).

New Labour's attitude towards children and young people generally provides a useful example of its fragmented approach to policy making: what is it that is being promoted – rights or responsibilities, care or control? The relatively recent shift in policy and practice towards rights and children's agency means that children's welfare is paramount and their voices are important (Prout et al, 2006). It seems the case that some aspects of legislation – the 1995 Children (Scotland) Act and the 2006 Childcare Act (England and

Wales) – and policy – *For Scotland's Children* (Scottish Executive, 2001a) and *Every Child Matters* (DfES, 2004) – are particularly child-friendly. The rights agenda, though, faces challenges from other aspects of current legislation and policy. There is now a growing emphasis on the extent to which children should be held responsible for their own behaviour – if they have rights and they are social agents, they also have responsibilities as 'good citizens' (Lister et al, 2005).

The youth justice arena is also characterised by a rights and responsibilities contradiction. As Goldson and Muncie (2006, p 203) suggest, the tension is very apparent:

> There is little coherence within the broader corpus of policy with regard to children and young people, and there is an uneasy relation, if not distinct fracture, between the correctionalist priorities that typify youth justice policy and the more inclusive and benign rationales that are said to characterise other core dimensions of state policy.

With children being viewed as directly responsible for their own behaviour, the implications in terms of offending is that we should not make excuses for them (Muncie, 2004). It is likely that justice and punishment models, where court proceedings take only minimal account of age, stage or other mitigating circumstances, and any punishment meted out must be seen to fit the crime, will come to dominate (Goldson, 2002; Muncie, 2004). This will be irrespective of the extent to which children and young people who are involved in offending are among our most emotionally and socially deprived 'citizens' (Goldson, 2002; White and Cunneen, 2006). In the UK, England has so far adopted an especially punitive approach to children who offend (Goldson and Muncie, 2006) but Scotland appears to be catching up fast, despite the traditional 'needs and not deeds' approach of the Scottish Children's Reporter Administration (McAra, 2006).

Police-recorded crime statistics, as well as victim and self-report studies (Muncie, 2004), indicate that children are disproportionately involved in criminal behaviour and, certainly, the 'age–crime curve'[3] is a phenomenon whose existence is long established in criminological circles (Quetelet, 1996 [1842]). While an age–crime curve is difficult to dispute in itself, the fact that it is based on official statistics leaves it open to some challenge. Changes in law enforcement and in what the law counts as crime make it difficult to accurately measure whether crime is rising or falling. The growth in mass surveillance techniques means that more crime is likely to be discovered, especially in public places, which impacts more on young people. In contrast, many adult crimes are hidden (domestic and child abuse, fraud and embezzlement, state atrocities and illegal arms dealing) (Muncie, 2004). As Barry (2006, p 177) suggests:

> [T]he problem of youth offending … is not as extensive as politicians and the media would have us believe, and yet young people are bearing the brunt of increased political and media hype about a widespread and growing youth crime problem that can only seemingly be curtailed through increased and more punitive political directives.

Social work in neoliberal Britain

Price and Simpson (2007, p 29) argue that, since the beginnings of social work, 'the excluded' and 'the poor' have been the 'focus of intervention', which 'adds more weight to the argument' that 'social exclusion' has its origins in the organisation of society and more explicitly in a feature of industrial capitalism. Certainly, our examination of neoliberal Britain provides more than enough evidence to suggest that some of our most vulnerable citizens are now more 'excluded' and 'poorer' than they have been for some time. This recognition poses a real challenge for social work yet the profession would seem to be in a position now where it is particularly difficult for social workers to make any significant difference to the lives of service users and carers.

If we accept that Third Way politics have continued along much the same track as original neoliberalism, we are able to cast a critical eye over the multifarious nature of the political, economic and social changes that have taken place since the 1970s. It is now almost 30 years since the government of Margaret Thatcher began to dilute state welfare responsibilities, undermine the role of welfare professionals, allow the rich to become richer and marginalise the UK's poorest and most vulnerable individuals, groups and communities. This trend, we argue, has continued under New Labour and, as a result, the social work of now is very different to that of the 1970s. This is not to suggest that social work got it right in the 1970s – it did not, as Chapter Two outlines! – but rather to highlight the extent to which many social workers now do not recognise the job they are doing as bearing any relation to the profession they chose to enter (Jones, 2001, 2005; Lymbery, 2004). The work of Chris Jones (2001, 2005, 2007), in particular, assembles a strong case against neoliberal, managerial practices in social work. His research – most recently interviews with 40 frontline practitioners in England and discussions with similar workers in Wales and Scotland – discovered a depressing pattern, with staff experiencing physical and emotional exhaustion, stress, frustration and resentment. While Jones accepts that the demands of working with people in need are many, and can cause anxiety, his research found that the pressures felt by social workers came mainly from their agencies and not from service users. When conducting research for this book, we found state social workers to be similarly frustrated by what is happening to their jobs. As will be explored in more detail in the next chapter, workers were pulled away from direct work with service users, burdened by the emphasis on performance indicators, outcomes and inspections and at times deserted by senior managers intent on playing their own versions of the managerial game.

This apparent 'crisis' in state social work remains despite New Labour's attempts to recruit and retain social workers and its creation of Social Care Councils and Institutes for Excellence in a bid to raise standards in social work education, training and practice. Social work is now much more in the spotlight but the emphasis has tended to be on where social work has gone wrong and on why it needs to change. As we saw in Chapter One, *Changing Lives*, the 21st-Century Social Work Review in Scotland (Scottish Executive, 2006a, p 10), while recognising that social workers are committed, hard-working individuals, argued that 'more of the same won't work'. This suggests that social workers have been barking up the wrong tree all these years and need to change tack as a matter of urgency. Granted, the report notes that there are new social and personal needs to be met – mention is made of increasing social polarisation, for example – but it fails to link these new needs to almost 30 years of neoliberal, neoconservative economic and social policies. Instead, the report emphasises that there are new requirements and responsibilities that social work must rise to: the demands of a managerial, marketised public sector; the requirements laid down by the Social Care Councils and Institutes for Excellence; and the increased expectations of whole new layers of regulation and inspection. In short, although the report was endorsed both by the previous New Labour-led Executive in Scotland and by its Scottish National Party minority government successor, there is, as yet, little to suggest that centralised policy measures will lead social work out of the mess (Ritchie and Woodward, 2009: forthcoming).

The next three chapters examine in more detail the extent to which any positive future for social work lies, in the main, with practitioners, service users and carers. We now return briefly to Aileen's story, however, to reinforce one of our central arguments (to which we return in several of the forthcoming chapters): that good social work practice is radical practice. It *is* very tough for many practitioners and service users who struggle on in the current economic, political and social circumstances that we discuss in this chapter. It is this very state of affairs, though, that makes it more necessary now than before for social workers to embrace an approach to practice that is critical of existing structures and that reclaims ethical and value-based stances as its own.

Conclusion: Aileen's story

Aileen's appalling experiences of social work services in her second professional post reflect the key features of neoliberalism that were outlined in this chapter. There was an examination of the impact on UK society of both Thatcherite policies and New Labour's Third Way – in terms of the marketisation of public services, the increase in poverty and inequality and the unparalleled growth in public, political and media demonisation of particular groups in society. That its effects are broadly negative for the majority of us – and catastrophic for a significant minority – leaves us with an unpalatable sense of disempowerment, alienation, frustration and often anger. These feelings become particularly powerful when we remind ourselves that neoliberalism, despite its pernicious effects, has come to dominate political and public life. As Monbiot (2007) argues:

> Richard Nixon was once forced to concede that 'we are all Keynesians now'. Even the Republicans supported the interventionist doctrines of John Maynard Keynes. But we are all neoliberals now. Margaret Thatcher kept telling us that 'there is no alternative', and by implementing her programmes Clinton, Blair, Brown and the other leaders of what were once progressive parties appear to prove her right.

At the same time, and, as will be discussed in later chapters, neoliberal globalisation has provoked a 'tide of revolt' (Callinicos, 2003). We are seeing positive developments in the spread of anti-globalisation, anti-demonisation and pro-environmental movements (Callinicos, 2003; Curran, 2006) and, in social work, of critical, potentially radical, responses to service user oppression and practitioner demoralisation (Powell and Geoghegan, 2005; Ferguson and Lavalette, 2007a; Ferguson, 2008). For Aileen, it was her commitment to working within the state sector that finally spurred her on to make some changes. Her first professional post confirmed that, for her, social work is about working alongside the people who are experiencing social and personal problems of the most complex and damaging nature. Her preferred role is frontline social worker, supporting, advising, helping, listening to and responding to children and families, often with multiple needs. While her responsibilities rightly expect that the care and support she provides is delivered at times within tight legal requirements – she is fully aware of when she has to act to protect children, for example – she remains certain that these responsibilities can be discharged without resorting to unethical or oppressive practice. It might have been easier for Aileen to leave her second employer but she chose to stay and, in her own words, 'fight for change'. This is what she has done so far:

- She has become a shop steward for UNISON, the trade union she has been a member of since her student days. She now has responsibility for recruitment and for supporting social work union members who are facing difficult or inequitable employment conditions.
- She has joined the local practitioner forum in the process of being established under the auspices of the 21st-Century Review in Scotland. Although rather sceptical about the Review process itself, and its aftermath, Aileen is clear that she needs to join with others if she is to have any hope of influencing the future of social work in the direction she would prefer.
- She has insisted with her line manager that supervision includes, instead of case counting and case allocation, a focus on the needs and rights of service users and carers and on her own continuing professional development.

At this stage, Aileen is acutely aware that she still has few opportunities to work alongside service users and carers. She is keen to work with interested colleagues to establish a programme to improve user and carer involvement in the planning and evaluation of services but her managers are insisting that the evaluation forms in place just now are sufficient. She still hopes, though, that her demands for more effective supervision will help her to look at her own practice with a critical perspective and consider ways in which she can work more creatively and flexibly, where she can emphasise the caring rather than authoritarian side to her role.

Aileen is making progress but it remains to be seen whether her commitment to the state sector can be maintained when her struggle is mainly an uphill one. As we will see in the next chapter, Aileen is not alone. Other state social workers do what they can, whenever they can, to hold on to the ideals that brought them into the profession in the first place. While the constraints are many, equally the possibilities are increasingly apparent.

Notes

[1] Similar economic and social shifts took place in other countries around the same time but on the back of military force (Argentina for example; Grassi and Alayón, 2005) or International Monetary Fund machinations (The Philippines for example; Harvey, 2005) rather than with popular consent as in the UK and the US.

[2] Rarely, however, did frontbench New Labour Members of Parliament seek to explain why social and personal problems had grown conspicuously during 18 years of Conservative government.

[3] The onset of criminal behaviour increases rapidly during late childhood and early adolescence and reaches its peak at about ages 17 or 18 for boys and 15 for girls (approximately 80% of child offenders are male). Involvement in crime then tapers off as maturity increases, by the early twenties for most.

Questions for discussion

➲ In what ways have the needs of the UK's most vulnerable people, service users among them, become increasingly complex in recent years and why might this worrying shift have occurred?

➲ Why are the rights of particular individuals, groups and communities being increasingly disregarded?

➲ Why are some social work managers so concerned with budgets, targets and outcomes yet so untroubled by overworked, disillusioned and alienated practitioners?

Suggestions for further reading

➲ Harris, J. (2003) *The Social Work Business*, London: Routledge. A highly critical consideration of the marketisation of social work and its current operation as a 'quasi-business'.

➲ Harvey, D. (2005) *A Brief History of Neoliberalism*, Oxford: Oxford University Press. Sums up neatly and accessibly the emergence of neoliberalism in the 1970s and explores its devastating economic and social consequences.

➲ McDonald, C. (2006) *Challenging Social Work*, Basingstoke: Palgrave Macmillan. Reflects on the numerous changes at policy and organisational levels that have affected the institutional context of social work. Although the damaging side of some of these changes is considered, the book is, fundamentally, optimistic: social work should not throw the baby out with the bath water but, equally, there are different ways in which social work can be understood and practised.

➲ UNICEF (United Nations Children's Fund) (2007) *Report Card 7, Child Poverty in Perspective: An Overview of Child Wellbeing in Rich Countries*, Florence, Italy: UNICEF Innocenti Research Centre, www.unicef-icdc.org/presscentre/presskit/reportcard7/rc7_eng.pdf. This report ought to have shamed British politicians into a major policy rethink in relation to children and young people. That it did not, shames them further!

State social work: constraints and possibilities

Box 4.1: 'Jenny'

The following quote is from 'Jenny', aged 33, who qualified as a social worker in July 2006. Her first job was in a local authority children's services team. Initially she worked on the 'help desk' (duty system) but was soon seconded to a new project looking to improve working relationships between social work and education:

> I was supposed to have an experienced social worker mentoring me ... but it became apparent quickly that, because of the level of work, she didn't have time. Also the community care worker who worked with us went off sick ... and never came back.... After Christmas, the senior mentoring social worker went on secondment and I was on my own for at least six weeks ... I was carrying a caseload of up to 23 cases, including eight child protection cases ... I was basically firefighting....
>
> There were at least two points in the first nine months when I woke up and thought about quitting.... The work itself has never been the issue. The issue is the organisation I work for being in a state of chaos, chopping and changing teams and parameters of work. I constantly felt I was just keeping my head above water. (Revans, 2008, p 15)

Introduction

'Jenny' was interviewed as part of a pilot study that explored the experiences of newly qualified statutory social workers in the South of England (Donnellan and Jack, 2008). The study found that newly qualified practitioners envisaged their role to be one of working directly with service users. Instead, they quickly became resentful and stressed when they found their work to be bureaucratic form filling, case recording and firefighting. Although contact with service users could be anxiety-provoking for these newly qualified workers, this did 'not translate into the same feelings of frustration as those produced by an employing organisation's demands' (Donnellan and Jack, 2008, p 15).

It is not hard to imagine why, after these experiences in her first qualified post, 'Jenny', and others like her, will be heading out the local authority door as quickly as possible. All 'Jenny' has seen is overwork, stress, lack of support and insufficient time to work closely with service users. Conversely, as we will see later in this chapter, the eight experienced workers who took part in our local authority social work focus group remained dedicated to statutory social work, at least in the medium term. First, they had seen the statutory sector in better days and, second, like Aileen from the previous chapter, they felt that statutory work continued to provide them with opportunities to work with some of society's most marginalised and vulnerable people. Certainly, they found themselves working in very restricted ways but they seemed optimistic that the situation in local authorities could and would improve. Similarly, the two newly qualified members of the statutory social work focus group had some positive experiences to report although they were sometimes overwhelmed by heavy workloads and bureaucratic demands.

This chapter explores the experiences of local authority social workers involved in what Jones (2001, 2005) has called 'state social work'. Later in the chapter we will discuss the possibilities for creative practice that currently exist, or that can be developed, within the state sector. We begin, however, with the constraints of working in this sector for the simple reason that, as we saw in the previous chapter and in 'Jenny's' account earlier, it is the state sector that appears most beleaguered due to persistent attacks on its efficiency and effectiveness and the increasingly demanding nature of the social and personal needs its workers are struggling to meet. Throughout, the chapter will draw on examples from statutory social work in the children and families, criminal justice and community care arenas.

Social work and the state

Chapter Two, while paying due respect to 1970s' and earlier radical ideas in social work, suggested that indiscriminate nostalgia for the good old days will do us little good. In the current climate, however, we can be forgiven for hankering after bygone days, especially when we remind ourselves that social work did succeed in making some real advances in the late 1960s and the 1970s, many of which have now been lost to the profession. A series of reforms occurred during this period, which were seen as truly progressive and which encouraged well-known social work academic Malcolm Payne (2005, p 85) to talk of 'social work at its zenith'. The state social work sector may have been strengthened during the 1950s and early 1960s on the back of wider welfare state reforms, but services continued to be fragmented and poorly coordinated in places. As a result, in 1965, the UK Labour government of Harold Wilson established a Committee, chaired by Sir Frederic Seebohm, to consider what changes were needed in England and Wales. Seebohm succeeded a similar Committee in Scotland, chaired by Lord Kilbrandon, which had reported in 1964 (Kilbrandon, 1964). Seebohm reported in 1968 (Seebohm, 1968) and, like Kilbrandon,[1] recommended the break-up of fragmented social services and their unification in new, generic local authority social services departments (social work departments in Scotland).

The philosophy of Kilbrandon and Seebohm was broadly universal – to provide a community-based service that was accessible and available to all rather than one that restricted itself to those most disadvantaged – and is summarised neatly in the following paragraph from the Seebohm Report:

> We recommend a new local authority department, providing a community-based and family-oriented service, which will be available to all. This new department will, we believe, reach far beyond the discovery and rescue of social casualties; it will enable the greatest possible number of individuals to act reciprocally, giving and receiving service for the well-being of the community. (Seebohm, 1968, para 2)

Grand words indeed, but words that captured something of the times in their emphasis on universality, community and reciprocity. With the publication of the Kilbrandon and Seebohm Reports, the 1968 Social Work (Scotland) Act and the 1970 Local Authority Social Services Act (England and Wales) were introduced, which lodged social work firmly within the state sector, with the voluntary sector being viewed as complementary and supplementary. The real advances of the time were seen most explicitly in: social work's new duty to assess needs and promote social welfare by providing services or, in some cases, financial assistance; the new Children's Hearing System in Scotland;[2] and the fresh emphasis on generic practice.

As Stevenson (2005) argues, alongside universalism, the notion of 'genericism' was important in this social work discourse of the 1960s and early 1970s. 'Generic' referred to the assumption that all social workers shared a common basis to their work – transferable knowledge, skills and values – and could, therefore, provide services for all as well as work in a range of ways and in a variety of contexts. The term 'generic', though, came to be much debated (Stevenson, 2005): can a generically trained social worker fully understand the particular needs of children, vulnerable adults and people who offend, and is it possible to practise effectively as a community worker, group worker and case worker? Despite the uncertainty surrounding the possibilities and problems associated with genericism, change was implemented swiftly. Social work's rapid growth in the state sector on the back of the welfare state, together with centralised requirements for education and training, provided a relatively new profession with the legitimacy it sought (Jones, 1999). The future seemed bright for social work, post-Kilbrandon and Seebohm, as it sought to embrace some progressive, potentially radical, ideas and to strengthen its professional status. The vision was for the profession to become a vital component of state welfare provision, where traditional case work would sit comfortably alongside community and group work models, generically trained workers would provide 'a universal service to respond to universal needs' (Horner, 2006, p 91) and the stigma associated with social work would be reduced.

'Where have all the good times gone?'

The reforms of the late 1960s saw social work take off within the state sector. Yet, little more than a decade later, the profession was under attack, from many different sides. This prompts the question, 'What happened?'. Why did the sheen come off state social work services so soon after they were established? For some, the answer may lie partly within social work itself. For example, in the 1970s, it became increasingly clear to more radical commentators that centralised, state-run social work services had done little to tackle, or to even highlight, the structural oppression that so blighted the lives of many service users. Questions began to be asked about social work's power and professionalism and its role in social control. Influenced by the feminist, black power and peace movements of the 1960s and 1970s (Webb and Wistow, 1987), which we discussed in Chapter Two, more 'emancipatory' approaches to practice began to develop (Dominelli, 2002b). Radical social work of the 1970s might not have overthrown the welfare state or established socialism in the UK but it highlighted the enduring nature of oppression – on the basis of social divisions such as class, gender, disability, ethnicity, age, sexuality and so on (Payne, 2006) – and the legitimacy of social justice as a goal for social work (Powell, 2001; Dominelli, 2002b).

While radical social workers of the 1970s argued that service users were structurally oppressed and socially marginalised, and that a core social work role was to advocate on their behalf, at no time did they suggest that social work needed anything but a strong place within the state welfare apparatus (Bailey and Brake, 1975). Social work continued to be governed by a strong 'social democratic consensus' that 'the public domain offered more of an opportunity for equal access to the provision of welfare and support services' (Carey, 2008, p 920). Yes, radicals criticised aspects of social work but their intention was to strengthen the profession's role in public services, in the interests of already marginalised social groups, not to undermine it. In the 1970s, however, the social work cause was not helped by one particular child abuse case. The death of Maria Colwell in 1973, following her return to the care of her mother and stepfather by social workers, drew attention to apparent failings in the social work system. Maria's social worker was blamed and humiliated and social work agencies were pilloried for being too soft (Corby, 2006). At the same time, questions began to be asked about the marked increase in the number of children being taken into state care, although it was not until the 1990s that evidence of institutional abuse began to emerge (Wolmar, 2000). Moreover, the rehabilitative ideals associated with social work in the adult and juvenile justice systems began to be seen as, at best, ineffective (by doing little, if anything, to tackle recidivism; Martinson, 1974) and, at worst, discriminatory (by pulling low-level offenders into the formal system unnecessarily and 'working' with them in unstructured and open-ended ways; McLaughlin and Muncie, 1993). It is fair to say, then, that there were problems within the state social work machine. It is equally important to recall that, as we saw in Chapters Two and Three, the fiscal crisis of the early 1970s led to cuts in public service funding, leaving social workers increasingly unable to provide the level of services required to meet growing social and personal needs.

By far the most damaging attacks on social work came instead from New Right politicians, led by Margaret Thatcher, and her media allies. As Chapter Three illustrates, attacks on public services from 1979 onwards were part and parcel of the assault on welfare that accompanied the neoliberal ascent. It did no harm at all to the neoliberal argument, however, to point the critical finger at social work in particular, accusing it of promoting 'political correctness', breeding dependence and wasting public money. In 1993, Jones and Novak (pp 195-6) wrote:

> Over the last fifteen years social work in Britain has undergone a significant transformation.... Facing a situation of increasing poverty and rising social stress, social workers have found themselves with even fewer resources to meet the needs of more desperate clients. At the same time, social work has faced increasing criticism and ridicule ... which have challenged its legitimacy and sense of identity.

Chapter Five may note that the voluntary sector has not escaped neoliberal reorganisation but it remains the case that state social work services in the UK have carried the brunt of persistent attempts by government, over the past 30 years or so, to 'modernise' public services to fit an agenda of residualisation, individualisation and privatisation. State social work, with little more than a whimper, has embraced the programme – begun by

UK Conservative politicians and developed by New Labour – to address welfare problems with business solutions (Farnsworth, 2006). As a result, social workers have become distanced from social work itself, from their professional values and ideals, and from the service users and carers who now need their support more than ever. The irony of this is all the more apparent when one considers the extent to which social work is actually a growth industry (Walton, 2005): there may be more social workers now but they remain 'swamped by demands' (Walton, 2005, p 589); our society may be richer now but social need is greater among the many who have missed out. Social work in the state sector is still there, despite threats of welfare state roll-back, and indeed state social work is a much larger arena now than it was 30 years ago. What is most apparent, however, is not the size of the state sector but the extent to which it has changed since the heady days of the late 1960s and early 1970s.

State social work realities

With social work being constructed increasingly as a failing profession, it is not surprising that governments wanted to be seen to respond formally, to lead this struggling profession into more 'efficient' and 'effective ways' of working. However, the changes imposed on social work in the past 30 years or so, and especially since 1997, come with little evidence that services have improved as a result.

Box 4.1: Living in an '-ation' nation

Fragmentation	Individualisation
Regulation	Bureaucratisation
Specialisation	Privatisation
Personalisation	Standardisation
Residualisation	Routinisation

There are indeed many '-ations' that could be said to characterise current practice realities in the state social work sector, most of them driven by neoliberal social and economic policies. While not all are necessarily negative – specialist services, for example, although they represent creeping fragmentation of social work, may also enable practitioners to respond to particular problems with greater levels of relevant knowledge and skills – the sheer number of '-ations' serves to highlight the extent to which social work in the state sector has been transformed, often not for the better.

As demonstrated in Chapter Three, both Conservative and New Labour politicians in the UK have had, at best, an ambivalent and, at worst, a destructive attitude towards social workers and service users (Jordan with Jordan, 2001). New Labour, in particular, has used the language of modernisation to introduce sweeping changes across the profession. As will be discussed later, however, some of the more conspicuous changes, although broadly welcomed by the social work profession because of their stated aim to improve the quality of services, are anything but 'benign' or 'benevolent' (McLaughlin, 2007). Rather, they have presided over increased 'state and employer regulation over workers' lives and are representative of a degraded view of social workers, their clientele and wider society' (McLaughlin, 2007, p 1264).

Regulation and standardisation: social work under surveillance

Conformity and control

Social work, generally, is now a much more regulated activity. As well as the central regulatory roles taken by the Institutes for Excellence and Social Care Councils (see later), inspection agencies now inspect and review social work services in a stated bid to improve efficiency and effectiveness. In England, there is the Commission for Social Care Inspection, which works closely with the Audit Commission and the Department of Health. In Scotland, there is the Social Work Inspection Agency, Audit Scotland and the Scottish Commission for the Regulation of Care.

Social Care Councils across the UK have begun to hold registers of staff working in the social care sector. In the case of qualified social workers, registration aims not only to protect their professional title – only those holding recognised qualifications and fulfilling other requirements can register as social workers – but also to regulate their conduct through codes of practice. How social workers ought to behave is now set in stone within codes of practice, giving rise to what McLaughlin (2007) describes as the '24/7 social worker', someone who is now under the gaze of colleagues, service users and the public at all times in their professional and private life. At the same time, however, the consultation process invoked prior to the introduction of the codes of practice demonstrated that workers and service users were broadly in favour of them. They were welcomed on the whole because they were likely to encourage 'appropriate' and 'competent' people into social care and to 'raise the profile of the profession' (GSCC, 2008).

Institutes for Excellence also emerged in England (2001) and Scotland (2003)[3] with a remit to identify and spread the word about what is 'knowledge-based good practice'. Between them the two UK-based agencies have released hundreds of guidance documents and tools to help workers, managers, educators, trainers, students, service users, carers and commissioners take forward research-based, good practice initiatives (SCIE, 2007a). The Institute in England states that over three quarters of a million people visited its website in 2006/07, and in Scotland some practice colleagues tell us that they appreciate the wealth of information now available to them via the Scottish Institute to help them develop their services. The increasingly key role being played by the Institutes raises two potential problems for us, however. First, we remain unsure about how independent of government, and how willing to criticise potentially inappropriate policy measures, these agencies are. The English Institute, for example, makes clear that its priority is to take forward 'the major policy issues such as personalisation of services, removing the stigma of mental illness, dignity in care, and listening to the carer voice' (SCIE, 2007a, p 3).

We welcome the thought of services becoming less stigmatised, more dignified and more in tune with the wishes of users and carers. We question, however, the central place now granted to personalisation ideas (Ferguson, 2007) and would like to have seen the Institutes more readily engage in critical debate. Generally, there is little to suggest that either the Institutes or the Social Care Councils are in the business of critically appraising dominant discourses, therefore it seems likely that they will take the profession in the direction government wishes it to go. Second, we remain sceptical about the way in which notions of evidence-based practice have taken hold across the profession. Increasing standardisation within social work is illustrated readily by this contemporary emphasis on evidence-based practice.

The future is evidence based

In 2001, Webb (2001, p 58) argued:

> The idea that good practice is ultimately to be delivered by research informed evidence which is underpinned by rigorous and effective methodologies is deeply appealing to our contemporary technocratic culture. Indeed evidence-based approaches are likely to gain even more salience in organizations, such as social services, where fiscal and resource crises are forcing human resource rationalizations, ever new restructuring strategies and increased monitoring of accountability through quality audits and control mechanisms.

The rise and rise of the evidence-based movement in social work is viewed by several commentators (Parton and O'Byrne, 2000; Butler and Pugh, 2004; Glasby and Beresford, 2006) as a key part of New Labour's agenda to find quick fixes for entrenched problems, based on an assumption that research can and does identify 'what works'. Raising questions about evidence-based practice as we do here is not to suggest that practice should not be based on sound knowledge about what approaches are likely to work more readily than others. To do otherwise would leave social workers providing hit-and-miss services, firing shots in the dark, and even more open to criticism. What we do question, however, is the uncritical assumption that evidence-based practice provides the answer to all, or at least most, service users' difficulties.

Glasby and Beresford (2006, pp 269-70) ask the same questions that we do:

> [W]hat constitutes valid evidence? Who decides? Do certain types of evidence seem to be treated as more legitimate than others? What happens when the evidence is fragmented or even contradictory? How much evidence does there need to be before we can confidently develop and roll out a particular policy?

Moreover, we consider that service users' evidence still struggles to gain equal ground with that of professionals and academics. As Branfield et al (2006) argue, service users' knowledge was instrumental in moving health and care agencies away from medical and towards social models of disability. This, however, is only one example and many barriers to accepting and using service users' evidence remain. Countless service users have limited chances to share and develop their ideas and views; professional and academic traditions and interests remain dominant.

Our main concern is what this hive of regulatory activity is actually doing for social workers and service users. As we will see later in this chapter, social workers are frustrated about the extent to which they are inspected – believing that it takes time and money away from service provision – and are sceptical about whether anything is improving as a result – they still feel overworked and undervalued and struggle to meet service users' needs. The core of our argument, which is supported by what practitioners tell us, and by our own experiences of state social work, is that supporting staff, and trusting them to do the job for which they were educated, is more likely to improve service quality than increased regulation.

One size fits all?

Direct practice, across the state and voluntary sectors, is now shaped by standardised and integrated assessment frameworks, risk assessment models and 'do and don't' checklists, which, of course, it is argued, are based on reliable, research-based evidence. Taking work with children and families as an example, practitioners across the health, social work and social care spectrum are encouraged to use the Common Assessment Framework in England (CWDC, 2007) and the Integrated Assessment Framework in Scotland (Scottish Executive, 2005). Similarly, in Scotland, the Single Shared Assessment (SSA) of community care needs was introduced following the publication of a report on the then New Labour government's Joint Future agenda (Scottish Executive, 2000). The SSA aims to unify what used to be separate processes for referral, assessment, planning and intervention, run by social work, nursing, occupational therapy and physiotherapy departments, into one shared process.

Service users most likely appreciate not being assessed time and time again. Indeed, research suggests that standardised approaches to assessment in children and families social work, for example the Framework for the Assessment of Children in Need and their Families (DH, 2000), are appreciated by some service users, as long as the forms are used by skilled and sensitive practitioners in therapeutic and creative ways (Charles with Wilton, 2004; Miller and Corby, 2006). In the current climate of higher and higher eligibility, however, there is no guarantee that one superbly conducted assessment will result in users and carers receiving the services that they need and wish; the needs-led, but resource-curtailed, environment would seem to prevail (Garrett, 2003; McDonald, 2006; McDonald et al, 2007).

Overly standardised and bureaucratised approaches to practice in many cases marginalise the important personal qualities that service users so appreciate in their social workers. As will be discussed in more detail in Chapter Six, service users expect social workers to have a range of skills but form-filling expertise is not one of them. Over the years, service users and carers have stressed that what they appreciate in social workers is an ability to be respectful, supportive, encouraging, reassuring, patient, attentive, empathic, warm, honest, trustworthy and reliable (Skinner, 2001; Institute of Applied Health and Social Policy, 2002; Aubrey and Dahl, 2005; Beresford, 2007; Cree and Davis, 2007; Doel and Best, 2008).

Box 4.2: Kate's story

A service-user-led seminar held at Stirling University in 2007 had student social workers laughing and cringing in equal measure. Kate is a qualified social worker but also a parent juggling mental health problems, the care of a disabled child and financial difficulties. She was able to catalogue for students her numerous and increasingly farcical encounters with form-filling, pen-wielding, unyielding and unsympathetic bureaucrats from the local social services department.

Two and a half years later and her family still receives no formal social work support. Despite being entitled to services for their disabled child, nothing has materialised. Kate, her partner and their children continue to struggle, relying totally on their own resources, which, at times, are just not enough. As Kate's story unfolded, students witnessed her frustration, anger, stress and resilience. While students' empathy with her circumstances will not change matters for Kate in the short term, she was encouraged by their ability to learn from her experiences.

Students commented:

- on the problems with care management approaches to practice – assessment produced an acknowledgement that Kate's family is in need but did not guarantee that services were then provided;
- that, in Kate's case, assessment was used to determine individuals' and families' eligibility for services and then to ration the scarce services available;
- that assessments were based on form filling and provided few opportunities for workers to build relationships with Kate and her family;
- that workers appeared to be intimidated by Kate's professional status and to assume a defensive air – this led students to note that, if Kate, a qualified social worker and an articulate, knowledgeable woman, cannot obtain the services she needs, particularly isolated and marginalised individuals and families are likely to struggle much more;
- on the need for their own practice to reflect both traditional values based on respect, empathy and non-judgemental attitudes, and emancipatory values based on recognition of structural oppression, inequality and professional power.

Paperwork, not people

It is not just service users and carers who rue the loss of focus on relationship-building and the emphasis on bureaucracy. *Changing Lives*, the 21st-Century Review of Social Work in Scotland (Scottish Executive, 2006a) discovered a majority of social workers who reported that the heart had gone out of their social work practice, especially in the state sector; that they had become increasingly distanced from the broadly altruistic reasons that took them into the profession in the first place. When examining this in more detail, it is apparent that the report's findings echo what some have been arguing for several years (Jones and Novak, 1993; Jones, 2001, 2005; Audit Commission, 2002; Harris, 2003; Ferguson and Lavalette, 2004; McDonald et al, 2007) – that marketisation and managerialism, under the umbrella term of modernisation, have 'systematically reshaped and effectively rebranded' (Stepney, 2006, p 1290) social work.

In terms of social work with adults, research suggests that practice has become increasingly routinised and standardised (McDonald et al, 2007). Now in place are bureaucratic systems, performance management, and supervision focused on procedures rather than professional development, all of which illustrate the extent to which social work is now regulated according to externally imposed criteria. Also, criminal justice social work in Scotland, and the National Offender Management Service (NOMS)[4] in England and Wales – arguably more so than other specialist areas of practice because the attentions of government, media and the wider public remain focused on crime and anti-social behaviour – have been subjected to increased scrutiny and additional demands to adopt a 'one size fits all' approach (Robinson and Burnett, 2007). With even more standardised risk assessment frameworks than exist in either children and families or adult services (Barry, 2007), and an often blanket emphasis on the 'what works' orthodoxy (Smith, 2004), criminal justice practice sometimes struggles to provide the 'inclusive and collaborative' (Gorman et al, 2006), relationship-based approaches that research suggests are a key component in all work with people who offend (McNeill et al, 2005). At the risk of repeating ourselves, it is important to emphasise that social work services ought to work for users and carers. As Glasby and Beresford (2006, p 269) ask, 'Who could possibly argue that what we do in public services should not be based on what we know to work?'. To provide community-based services for people who offend that work – that aim to reduce the risk of reoffending and satisfy demands for public safety – has to offer much more than a narrow emphasis on cognitive intervention, however. As one Scottish criminal justice worker said: 'I would argue strongly that some people require an intervention that is *welfare* oriented. To deny that is discriminatory' ('Ron', cited in Cree and Davis, 2007, p 50; emphasis in original).

Social work education

Within social work education the relatively new BA degree is based on a standardised set of outcomes for all (DH, 2002a; TOPSS, 2002; Scottish Executive, 2003), as was the Diploma in Social Work (DipSW) before it. The DipSW was sometimes criticised for its emphasis on social work training rather than on education (Preston-Shoot, 2004), for its rather narrow view of what social work is (Preston-Shoot, 2000, cited in Preston-Shoot, 2004, p 686) and for its potential to undermine autonomy and flexibility in practitioners with its competence-based approach (Dominelli, 2002c; Lymbery, 2003). In some ways, the new degree represented an attempt to come to grips with the complex nature of the social work role and task and, particularly in England, with its increasing association with social care (Orme, 2001). Instead of the DipSW's 26 single competences, the new degree is based on a set of standards each requiring that students demonstrate not just that they have gained competence in a particular area but also that they have acquired set knowledge and skills. To ensure that students are able to achieve the new standards, academic institutions are required to deliver a fairly prescribed degree programme, based on set teaching, learning and assessment requirements (Eadie and Lymbery, 2007), in relation to service user and carer involvement and integrated working practices, for example (DH, 2002a). In trying to reflect the complexity of social work, however, the new degree's benchmarking statement now contains 80 learning outcomes (Jackson, 2001, cited in Burgess, 2004), which ensures that its implementation is an extremely complex process. As Burgess (2004) notes, at least the learning outcomes and standards have been combined into one framework document in Northern Ireland, Wales and Scotland, making the requirements in these three countries a little more manageable than those in England.

While there is scope for locally negotiated agreements about the content and delivery of social work degree programmes (Preston-Shoot, 2004), broadly the knowledge, skill and value base that educators must teach, and students must acquire, is externally imposed. This would be fine if we were all in agreement about what good social work (or good social work education) is, but we are not (Preston-Shoot, 2004). Also, as Burgess (2004) suggests, developing a good curriculum requires educators to consider factors over and above the requirements of external agencies or internal quality procedures, for example, student needs, student time, research interests, costs and internal aims and objectives. That competence-based approaches can be combined with more creative and critical approaches to social work education, to ensure that students acquire more than just training by numbers, is apparent (Lymbery, 2003; Eadie and Lymbery, 2007; Fook and Askeland, 2007). Our own experiences in Scotland suggest, though, that lecturers struggle at times to cover all aspects of the new degree *and* to support students to think critically, politically and creatively, while students themselves have relatively few opportunities to develop their own interests and approaches to practice.

State social work has seen its status and its priorities change markedly since the reforms of the late 1960s. During this 40-year period it has received numerous makeovers, some progressive, but many less so. Social work continues to grow but, arguably, its development has stalled. What we see now is an assumption that all aspects of management, practice and education require external control. The developments discussed earlier are promoted almost as panaceas, which will ensure that services are consistent, accountable, effective and efficient. To what extent, however, can this controlled and controlling climate support practice that is sufficiently creative and flexible to respond to complex and fluid human needs? To what extent also, do such measures become the proverbial stick with which to beat hard-pressed social workers who do not shape up as required? As Webb (2001, p 76) notes in relation to evidence-based practice, 'social work requires a model that is much more nuanced and sensitive to local and contextual factors'. The 'one size fits all' approach continues to dominate policy statements, however, and practice has become increasingly bureaucratic and routinised as a result.

Working on the frontline: voices of state social workers

So why do some workers stick with state social work? What do they feel they contribute to it and receive from it? To help us explore the current constraints within the state social work sector, and to assess whether spaces still exist for workers to practise at all flexibly, critically or even radically, we invited 10 social workers to contribute to a focus group discussion. The workers were based in seven different local authorities across Scotland and worked in children and families, adult and youth justice and adult (community care) services as practitioners, managers and practice teachers. They were (all names of the people who took place in focus groups have been changed to protect anonymity): Murray, qualified for 16 years, who manages youth justice services; Valerie, qualified for 10 years, with a background in both adult and children's services and current responsibilities in practice teaching; Amy, qualified for 20 years, who has held a variety of jobs in children's services and remains a frontline practitioner and active practice teacher; Robert, qualified for 14 years, who is now a frontline manager in children's services; Mary, qualified for one year, who is based in children's services but who is also a highly experienced youth worker; Craig, qualified for 19 years, who has spent over 15 years in criminal justice services and is now a frontline manager; Kathryn, qualified for eight months, who is based in a joint disabilities team (working alongside health professionals); Conor, qualified for 30 years, who is a frontline manager in generic social work services; Melanie, qualified for seven years, who works in adult criminal justice services; and Frances, qualified for 12 years, who is a full-time practice teacher but who has worked in adult services in both the state and voluntary sectors.

'That's another fine mess you've gotten us into'

Most of these workers had relatively long-standing associations with the state social work sector, and emphasised their commitment to it. Most had chosen to stay in state social work but, whether highly experienced or relatively newly qualified, workers were in broad agreement about the constraints they faced on a daily basis. Significantly, none spoke of service users or carers as causing them problems, in spite of their recognition of growing social and personal need among the UK's already marginalised groups. By contrast, the obstacles in the way of good practice were perceived to be political and organisational. Robert, for example, felt that practice was driven by political demands for accountability and best value, which were anything but compatible with either good management or good practice:

> '[T]his whole exercise is to meet the needs of the political masters but what this means for workers is that different sections of management ... are in competition ... if one person protects their budget it is usually at the expense of someone else.'

He continued:

> 'The managers control day-to-day practice, which is just chasing numbers and chasing targets.'

At the same time, external attempts to make workers effective, through performance indicators and set outcomes, were seen as politically driven but bearing no relation to good practice. In Conor's words:

> 'We live in a performance framework where outcomes have to be seen to be measured. I think we all know that outcomes are really very, very difficult to measure but nevertheless they are measured, a lot of them are measured in such meaningless ways.'

External inspection was also seen as placing social work under surveillance in unhelpful and demoralising ways. For Kathryn the whole inspection process was about how local authorities "look externally to the assessors" rather than about improving services to meet the needs or promote the rights of either staff or service users. Murray also noted the extent to which everything stops to ensure that the inspectors are impressed, despite the lack of evidence to suggest that inspection actually improves practice:

> '[T]he local authority seems to put out a red carpet for the inspectors and to treat the people who are running around getting all the stuff for them with contempt ... we need to research this aspect of inspection, because it has not necessarily been established that it raises standards.'

Every aspect of social work was seen now as a legitimate area for inspection, prompting Valerie to say: "now we've got somebody in doing a pee inspection!". This emphasis on measurement and inspection was seen to have had a real impact on social workers because it left them constantly looking over their shoulders, waiting for someone to say that they were not working hard enough or smart enough. As a result, workers struggled to either use or retain their social work skills, knowledge or values and service standards deteriorated. For Robert, workers were less confident in their own abilities:

> 'What's missing is the opportunity for staff to do the job as they want to be able to.... What falls off the agenda is very good skilled and well-equipped individuals.'

Kathryn too noted a loss of emphasis on anything that could be classed as good practice in adult services:

> 'What we do is the lowest common denominator, it's the minimum that [people] need to be safe.'

Similarly, Melanie was staggered by how little time she had in which to complete reports for the court in criminal justice services, while noting that, as a newly qualified worker, she had something of a protected workload:

> '[Y]ou're talking about working in a person-centred way, supporting the rights of the service user, but you're knowing that you have only an hour and a half ... to do an SER [Social Enquiry Report].'

Mary finds herself in a situation very similar to that faced by Aileen, our social worker from the previous chapter. For Mary, social work with children and families provides few opportunities to develop good practice because there is neither enough time nor sufficient numbers of experienced staff left from whom she can learn:

> 'Workers can sometimes feel they've not got an opportunity to develop themselves or share their experiences ... workers are there for two or three years and they're off.'

For Craig, also in criminal justice social work, this lack of time to build good practice and to secure support from colleagues was an omnipresent problem for practitioners and managers. It was seen as a problem of staffing and therefore a higher-level responsibility but one that came back to bite frontline workers in particular:

> 'There simply isn't enough staff to do the job to the level that they're being asked to do it.... We need time to work to a high standard and at the moment we don't have that so we cut corners ... and it seems to me it's been mainly workers … it's been people in the frontline who have taken the rap when things go wrong.'

Instead of recognising where corners were being cut, however, social workers emphasised senior management's inability or failure to accept where problems in service provision lay. Conor stressed the extent to which he was required by his management to flag up unmet needs but to no avail:

> 'I've never known anybody come back to me and say, "Oh, we've been looking at your unmet need and we're really worried about it and we've decided we're going to give you more resources" ... it's just another performance indicator that's absolutely ludicrous!'

In some local authorities it seems that there have been attempts to plug gaps in services but this was proving an additional source of stress for frontline workers. Robert was particularly vexed about this:

> 'What has happened is that people [social workers] become brokers … where they're farming stuff out, contracting other agencies in the voluntary sector and the private sector ... they in turn are lower paid, possibly less motivated, workers who are coming into a situation they're unaware of.'

Generally, the state social workers interviewed in the focus group discussion emphasised a tension between political and management priorities on the one hand and practice priorities on the other, which left workers feeling exposed, undervalued, deskilled and deprofessionalised. In Robert's words:

'There's a huge gap between managers ... who are trying to
implement what we've been talking about and their understanding
of what actually good social work practice is.'

Most apparent in our discussion with state social workers, however, was their
dedication to social work. Whether long-term or recently qualified, workers
stressed their determination to stay in social work; none was thinking of
leaving the profession outright. What was particularly encouraging, though,
was that the survival urge was clearly linked to a strong commitment to
service users, rather than to meeting the demands of politicians and senior
managers. Social workers were still in social work for overwhelmingly
unselfish and humane reasons. Although admitting to struggling at times
in their fight to retain at least aspects of good practice, this struggle seemed
to be making them feel angry and resolute when they could, very readily,
have been crushed.

As a result, we are able to offer some alternatives to counter the doom and
gloom, which, unfortunately, we have had little choice but to emphasise so
far. The social workers who took part in our focus group might have been
weary of relentless change for change's sake but so too were they able, and
willing, to identify a more beneficial and constructive approach to practice
in the state sector.

'How we'd like to see it done': state social workers go radical

The workers who contributed to the focus group discussion highlighted
eloquently some of the pressures and limitations with which they have to
struggle in the state sector. Anyone standing on the outside and looking into
state social work might consider worker stress to be primarily associated with
their having to deal with difficult, unwilling and sometimes aggressive service
users. Equally, they might believe the anxiety to be linked to the difficult
decisions that have to be made, for example: whether to separate an abused or
neglected child from their parents; whether to suggest a community disposal
in the case of serious or persistent offending; or whether to support the
compulsory admission to hospital of someone experiencing mental ill-health.
As illustrated earlier, however, in both 'Jenny's' account of her first qualified
job and the experiences of focus group members, the demands placed on
workers as a result of unrelenting policy, organisational and managerial
change are more detrimental to social workers' well-being than are the
challenges posed at times by work with service users and carers.

It is to a discussion of the possibilities for more critical and creative practice
within the state sector that this chapter now turns. Again, the words of social

workers will be used to illustrate the extent to which practitioners do not just survive social work but labour daily to keep the needs and rights of service users and carers at the heart of their practice. This is not to suggest that state social workers are under any delusions about the complexity of the work they are involved in; while most come into the profession to help, equally they recognise that helping some might mean controlling the behaviour of others.

In Craig's words:

> 'There are restrictions with criminal justice and it's not an equal relationship but a relationship based on orders approved by courts ... so you can't pretend to work completely collaboratively ... but the relationship is still at the heart of it ... you build up a relationship first, you find out what really is at the heart of this person's problems and then you try to work out a shared strategy to address that.'

As stated earlier, the focus group consisted of committed and tenacious workers, all of whom saw possibilities for a different social work practice. The comments that follow were generated in response to the question 'What might radical (or a more resistance-based) social work look like in the first decades of the 21st century?'. Workers here spoke of their broad commitment to building relationships with services users, to recognising the impact of structural oppression and to finding some time to come together with like-minded colleagues in a bid to defend social work values.

For Conor, radical practice, both in the 1970s and today, is associated with practice that is generic and community oriented, an approach that he and his team colleagues strive to retain:

> 'It's very, very important that we're not fragmented and over-specialised ... our ability to go out to the community and network with people right across the board is extremely valuable and a small radical practice because nobody else is doing it anymore ... we should be looking to get back to that.'

Conor was aware that the rural setting in which he works perhaps lends itself to generic working and to approaches that are in tune with the needs of the local community. For Craig, however, it is the specialist nature of criminal justice services that has improved services for people who offend because:

> 'I, as a generic worker, was effectively a children and families worker and ... the demands on the service were such that they [children]

took priority over everything else ... there was no criminal justice service ... specialisation definitely has improved things.'

Craig recognised, however, the extent to which specialised teams actually pull against one another:

'There's something missing at senior level in recognising that we really need to work hand in hand and sometimes it feels like we're actually fighting against each other.'

Generally, senior managers came in for a high level of criticism from focus group members but Frances had one example of more creative practice at a senior level:

'A service user was involved in high-profile offending in the community and was causing a lot of concern ... but behind that was a very damaged young man.... At a children's hearing[5] ... because of the high-profile response to young people who are now being demonised and marginalised ... an Anti-Social Behaviour Order [was made] ... to force the local authority to move him outside the community. Fortunately, the local authority responded at a high level to challenge that ... supporting the young person and the worker to argue for the young person to remain in the local community. It was nice to see managers supporting a young person ... in a meaningful way, in a way that is consistent with social work, rather than having a knee-jerk reaction and saying "Let's get him out!".'

Similarly, Kathryn's own team manager was fully supportive of attempts to speak up for the rights of oppressed service users within adult services:

'Our team has very strong social work values ... we're unafraid to challenge the internal system and we have an excellent manager as well so we can see ourselves as a force ... insisting on creating that kind of dialogue.'

In returning to the idea of community-based approaches, as promoted earlier by Conor, Robert could see a strong argument for them too but felt that his large, urban local authority had lost sight of this for the time being. Instead, he argued that reclaiming skilled practice was one way in which to offer a potentially radical approach in the current climate:

'[W]e've won the idea that being a skilled worker is actually pretty radical, you know.'

For Amy, any radicalism in practice was taking personal responsibility for her own practice, to ensure that she both looked after herself and remained focused on service users' needs:

> 'If we don't take some kind of personal responsibility then we just become more insulated, more depressed and more demoralised and to me that's kind of what radical practice is, it's not allowing yourself to get demoralised and maintaining a sense of focus.'

For several members of the group, radical ideas in practice were best illustrated in their individual work with service users, through the relationships they built with them, the attention they paid to their needs and rights and in their own, personal recognition of the oppression and discrimination they faced. For others, though, radicalism was more about joining together with individuals and groups in a variety of ways. For Conor, this was about working directly alongside members of the local community:

> '[W]e should be getting in alongside people in other agencies and people in communities to challenge oppression and challenge the way our lives are run for us by politicians.'

Similarly, for Kathryn, radicalism was about joining with service users and team colleagues to:

> 'transform the systems that you interact with.... If you see yourself merely as one cog within the machine then you have no power whatsoever.'

Chapters Six and Seven will explore the possibilities for bringing together workers and service users. In the focus group, however, collective action was viewed more often than not as an opportunity for workers to come together. There was plenty of discussion about the fairly new practitioners' forums, which were established in Scotland under the auspices of the 21st-Century Review of Social Work[6] (Scottish Executive, 2006a). Broadly, though, workers were suspicious of the government's agenda, seeing it as 'top-down' and 'remote' from practitioners' real-life concerns. It was recognised, however, that the 21st-Century Review process itself had provided social workers with some additional space in which to share aspects of good practice. The preferred approach, though, was for workers to do it by themselves, either through informal workplace meetings or trade unions, rather than to attend externally organised practitioners' events.

In Valerie's authority, there had been several positive steps taken:

'[W]e've managed to establish a social work forum for workers who meet every couple of months and at the last one we were looking at the number of people from Eastern European countries who have come to the [X] area ... we've gradually, by just coming together, been surprised about how many people there now are and about the conditions they are living in so we're using that forum to think of [proposals] to take back to our managers ... I think we're lucky to be given the space to do that given our workloads.'

Frances was equally keen on bringing social workers together:

'That type of set-up is very helpful for sharing ideas, sharing innovative practice, sharing creative practice.'

For Murray, anything that involved "extracting social workers from their relationships with their computers", like the practitioners' groups described by Valerie and Frances above, was to be viewed positively. He was clear, though, that these groups could not be too confined to individual teams or local authorities because the point was "to work on behalf of social work and to use any opportunity to affect policy".

It seems that social workers do many things to counteract the forces of managerialism:

- provide support to each other;
- develop their practice by sharing innovative approaches;
- maintain their individual commitment to professional values – several focus group members had attended the Social Work: A Profession Worth Fighting For? conferences in Liverpool (2006) and Glasgow (2007);
- focus on building strong and meaningful relationships with service users and carers;
- advocate with and for marginalised and oppressed groups and individuals;
- seek to influence policy in the interests of workers, service users and carers.

Several belonged to strong teams, had helpful managers and were linked in with practitioners' groups that they found supportive. Some too were willing to speak up, to take concerns to senior management and, if need be, to say, 'No!'. For most of the focus group members, however, social work remained a fairly individualised task; people did their best within their own agency setting, and according to their particular roles, to support users, carers, students and colleagues with whose needs they strongly identified. This said, the focus group members remained members of their relevant trade union, although they recognised an increasing 'depoliticisation' of social work, which, to a person, they deeply regretted.

Murray, for example, was adamant about the key role to be played by the trade union:

'[N]ot being in the union in social work seems hazardous to me.'

Amy and Frances linked this perceived loss of political awareness both to the way in which student social workers are educated today and to wider social forces that emphasise individual responsibility and, at times, blame:

'I've certainly noticed a difference in people coming out of colleges and universities in terms of understanding the bigger picture.' (Amy)

'The new standards that we're working to [in social work education] ... don't explicitly mention anti-oppressive practice.' (Frances)

Craig wondered whether age too was a factor:

'[The last time I was on strike] the only people who crossed the picket were children and families ... and community care ... the only people on the picket line were criminal justice and admin ... and I was thinking "What's going on here?" and the only thing I could come up with was the [youthful] age of the workers.'

Both Murray and Amy, with over 35 years of qualified service between them, and newly qualified, still youthful, Melanie, however, made a direct link between Thatcherism in the UK and the depoliticisation of social work. For example:

'[I]t was a shock to me having Thatcherism and working where you couldn't be political ... the consequences of politics are around for us all to see ... they [politicians] drive the climate now.' (Murray)

The focus group members could not, however, pinpoint a date when social work as they thought they knew it began to change so completely for the worst. As a result, they acknowledged the devious way in which modernisation has been accomplished. What is clear from state social workers is that it is only when they find time and space to think about their working lives that they begin to fully conceptualise what has been happening to them, to service users and to public services generally. Unfortunately, this chapter has demonstrated that precious little space to think and reflect in this way is available to workers within the state sector. What happens, then, is that the modernisation programme, which actually damages workers and service users rather than improves matters for them, is accepted relatively unquestioningly. Before workers know it, practices that once would have concerned them deeply become firmly established in the very fabric of social work.

It comes as an enormous relief, then, to hear directly from state social workers about their compassion for people who are struggling and their commitment to retaining aspects of practice that go some way towards meeting the needs and rights of service users and carers. In 2004, John Clarke suggested that, despite the dynamism of the neoliberal agenda, and the extent to which the public realm was under attack, public services continued to exist and, indeed, to work as a buffer against the most destructive elements of neoliberalism:

> For many reasons, the public realm (and the attachments that it mobilises) is part of the 'grit' that prevents the imagined neoliberal world system functioning smoothly. It makes a difference to our view of the world if we start by looking for the grit – taking notice of recalcitrance, resistance, obstruction and incomplete rule – rather than throwing them in as a gestural last paragraph after the 'big story' has been told. (Clarke, 2004, pp 44-5)

The social workers who took part in the state social work focus group for this book would probably not view themselves as particularly recalcitrant or obstructive but they certainly have plenty of 'grit' and resist in ways that work best for them and, where possible, for service users.

Conclusion: constraints and possibilities

The state sector contains many dedicated workers who try all sorts of approaches to keep their professional values and personal principles at the heart of their practice. It is, for many, an uphill struggle because of the extent to which the practice climate in the state sector has changed. Just revisiting the experiences of 'Jenny' from the beginning of this chapter provides us with all the evidence we need of the 'destabilising' changes (McDonald, 2006) that have driven some excellent workers away from statutory work in recent times. Escalating regulation and standardisation leave practitioners with little in the way of professional autonomy and few opportunities to practise in the flexible, creative and critical ways that they prefer, and which many increasingly marginalised and stigmatised service users and carers require. It seems to be the case, though, that workers have found ways not just to survive the state sector, but also to rise above its constraints. We did not find many examples of radical practice in its 1970s guise – for example, workers were not as yet joining service users in protests over the rising cost of electricity and gas (although as the recession bites perhaps they will find themselves doing so) – but we did hear about practitioners whose individual work was guided by their commitment to service users, much more than their commitment to agency procedure and government policy. In the current controlled and controlling climate, such practice can be seen as radical, even subversive.

Yet, focus group members were not undermining their agencies or putting their own needs first; they were doing their jobs and doing them well. All had progressed in their careers, several were committed practice teachers and all saw further opportunities to develop their knowledge and skills in social work. Individuals, though, tended to respond to work pressures in individual ways, leaving them feeling isolated at times and struggling to hold on to their ideals and principles.

The limitations of the state sector are there for all to see and to date official responses to improve the situation offer only a small light at the end of the tunnel. As yet we have no way of knowing whether or not the UK's reviews of social work will lead to more satisfying working environments for state social work staff or more positive experiences of service provision for users and carers. Indeed, as we were writing this book, it became increasingly clear to us that the way out of this mess is unlikely to be found by politicians and policy makers, who tend not to trust the profession. Solutions lie, rather, in practitioners, users and carers whose need for, and belief in, creative services is much more apparent.

Notes
[1] Kilbrandon also recommended the establishment of the Scottish Children's Panel (now known as the Scottish Children's Reporter Administration or SCRA; see www.scra.gov.uk/home/index.cfm).

[2] The Scottish Children's Hearing System, with its emphasis on children's needs rather than their deeds, was based on the assumption that both troubled and troublesome children had similar needs, which were rooted in family and community experiences. As a result, both children with care and protection needs, and those involved in offending or who displayed other behavioural problems, were to be dealt with in similar ways, before a Children's Panel rather than a Court. This, at the time, was seen as truly progressive.

[3] The Scottish Institute for Excellence in Social Work Education (SIESWE) became the Institute for Research and Innovation in Social Services (IRISS) in 2007.

[4] NOMS was established in 2004 to integrate the probation and prison services in England and Wales. This was in spite of strong opposition from

Napo, the trade union and professional association for probation and family court staff (Napo, 2005).

[5] In Scotland, the Scottish Children's Reporter Administration is responsible for conducting hearings in front of three lay panel members for children in need or in trouble. In England and Wales, children attend family or criminal courts. This example is not given to suggest that the children's hearing system deals more favourably with young people who offend than does a court-based system (indeed, this is an example of a punitive response by children's panel members). Rather, it is offered to illustrate that senior managers are not always hostage to the prevailing policy agenda.

[6] Two wide-ranging reviews of social work took place – one in Scotland in 2004/05 (Scottish Executive, 2006a) and one in England in 2005 (DoH/DfES, 2006). In Scotland, the report of the 21st-Century Social Work Review Team did well to recognise the extent to which social workers felt distant from service users and preoccupied with bureaucracy. It did little, however, to challenge the political and economic forces that had so undermined social work in the first place (Ritchie and Woodward, 2009: forthcoming).

Questions for discussion

- ⮩ Do the experiences of 'Jenny', the newly qualified social worker from the beginning of this chapter, sound familiar to you from your own place of work or practice learning opportunities? In what ways?
- ⮩ To what extent are state sector social workers still able to offer 'good' services to users and carers?
- ⮩ What do you consider to be the future of social work in the state sector?

Suggestions for further reading

➲ Carey, M. (2008) 'Everything must go? The privatization of state social work', *British Journal of Social Work*, 38 (5), pp 918-35. A lively critique of the 'political project' behind the creeping privatisation of social work in the state sector and of its 'considerable impact' on state social workers and people who receive social work services.

➲ Cree, V.E. and Davis, A. (2007) *Social Work: Voices from the Inside*, London: Routledge. Considers British social work in recent times from the perspectives of practitioners, service users and carers. The book is organised around six areas of social work practice and is, therefore, useful for highlighting current constraints and possibilities.

➲ Lymbery, M. and Butler, S. (eds) *Social Work Ideals and Practice Realities*, Basingstoke: Palgrave Macmillan. Although the difficulties faced currently by social workers are considered, this book is most helpful because it emphasises constructive ways forward. It aims to help workers to bridge the gap between the challenging realities of social work today and the ideals that brought them into the profession.

➲ McDonald, A., Postle, K. and Dawson, C. (2007) 'Barriers to retaining and using professional knowledge in local authority social work practice with adults in the UK', *British Journal of Social Work*, Advance Access, published 25 April. Based on recent research, this article suggests that the workforce in adult social care is both demoralised and demotivated. While problems at structural, managerial and practitioner level are considered, the emphasis is on the damage inflicted by neoliberal ideologies and managerialism.

The 'third sector': a radical alternative?

5

Box 5.1: Sandie

Sandie is a 34-year-old woman who completed her professional social work training two years ago. During her final placement, she worked in a small mental health voluntary organisation and enjoyed the opportunities this provided for working on a more equal footing with service users. These included involvement in an advocacy project, supporting a Hearing Voices group, and working with a group of service users to make a video about their lives. On qualifying, after a brief and unsatisfying period in a local authority community care team, where she felt she was not given the time or the opportunities to work with service users in the way she wanted, she took up a post in a mental health crisis team in a voluntary sector organisation. For the first year, she really enjoyed the work and the chance to explore what the social model of mental health meant in practice. Since then, however, the team, which receives most of its funding from the local authority, has been subjected to increasing financial cutbacks. As a result, there are now very few opportunities for staff training and the budget for involving service users in the project's management has been slashed. Project workers including Sandie, who are paid considerably less than local authority social workers and who have not received a pay increase for two years, have now reluctantly agreed to an extension of their working week from 35 hours to 37 hours. Most worryingly, senior management within the voluntary organisation have informed project staff that there is no budget for handover meetings during shift changes, something that Sandie feels is poor practice that could put service users at risk.

Introduction

During the 1990s, increasing numbers of social workers in Britain began to seek employment within voluntary sector organisations. Two factors contributed to this trend. One was the increase in job opportunities resulting from the huge expansion of the sector during this period. This expansion was based on the Conservative government's promotion of a 'mixed economy of care' following the implementation of the 1990 NHS and Community Care Act, a trend that has continued apace under New Labour. Thus, between 1991 and 2001, funding to the voluntary and community sector from government increased by nearly 40%. By 1999/2000, the amount of state funding received by the sector had grown to £1.1 billion (Paxton et al, 2005). The other factor attracting social workers, like Sandie in the example earlier, was a growing perception of the voluntary sector as a place where workers could practise in a way that was more consistent with social work values and ideals. In contrast to the local authority sector, voluntary organisations were increasingly seen as providing opportunities to do 'real' social work, in the sense of working directly with service users in more progressive ways.

There is more than a little irony here. While many voluntary organisations do now offer models of good practice, this has not always been the case. As we saw in Chapter Two, for much of its history the voluntary sector has been far from radical. The early Charity Organisation Society (COS), for example, richly merited Clement Atlee's description of it as an organisation 'essentially designed for the defence of the propertied classes' (cited in Lewis, 1995, p 86). Nor were other major voluntary organisations that dominated social work up until the Second World War always models of care and respect, let alone empowerment. Children's charities such as Dr Barnardo's and Quarriers' Homes, for example, along with many other voluntary organisations, were active participants in a scheme encouraged by the British government to reduce poverty at home by sending children from large families, orphanages or children living on the streets to the overseas dominions. Between 1869 and 1939, over 100,000 children were migrated from the UK to Canada by British philanthropic organisations. Although they were described – in the parlance of the Victorian era – as 'orphans, waifs and strays', in fact around two thirds had at least one surviving parent and most were from families experiencing extreme poverty. Once they arrived in Canada, the younger children were adopted, the older children committed as indentured labourers.

Box 5.2: Halifax and onwards

The majority of Quarriers' children disembarked at Halifax, Nova Scotia. On the quayside today on Pier 21 there is a museum commemorating the lives of all emigrants to Canada. In the museum there is a plaque that reads: 'In honour of the 100,000 British children, aged 6 to 14, orphans and non-orphans, who between 1859 and 1948 were shipped to Canada, where most worked as domestic servants and farm labourers'. The distinguished Professor of History

> who wrote the text for the plaque had wished to include the fact that the children were 'cheap farm labour' but was overruled by officialdom and feels that her message was 'neutered'.
>
> *Source:* IRISS (2008)

In this chapter, we will explore the role of the voluntary sector under New Labour governments since 1997 and assess what opportunities the sector offers for radical social work practice. As in the previous chapter, this will involve drawing on the views and experiences of a group of experienced frontline workers and managers, this time from voluntary sector organisations. One 'push' factor leading workers to view such organisations more positively – namely, the growth of managerialism in the local authority sector – has already been addressed in previous chapters and so will only be touched on here. Rather, the focus in this chapter will be on the main 'pull' factor, namely, the transformation in terms of both size and role of the voluntary sector since the early 1990s and the perception that it allows opportunities for more empowering practice, especially in respect of service user involvement.

So far, we have used the term 'voluntary sector'. In fact, in policy discussion, it is now more common to refer to the 'independent sector' or the 'third sector'. The change is more than a linguistic one. As Harris (2003, p 155) has noted, the independent sector, like the third sector:

> was a new term that embraced both commercial organisations and voluntary organisations, collapsing some of the previous distinctions between them and cloaking the embrace of the profit motive through use of private sector social services provision. As a result, the composition, management style and ethos of voluntary organisations were constrained to change.

The final part of this chapter will look briefly at the increasing role of the private sector in social work and social care and consider the extent to which private social work organisations are capable of challenging the structural inequalities and oppressions faced by many service users.

'A quiet revolution' – transforming the voluntary sector

Some indication of the distance travelled by voluntary sector organisations since New Labour came to power in 1997 was provided by the then

Chancellor of the Exchequer, Gordon Brown, in a keynote speech to the National Council for Voluntary Organisations' Annual Conference in early 2004:

> And over the last decade, from a time when you were much smaller, when there was no compact, when your professionalism was not properly recognised as it should be, we have witnessed what I believe … is your transformation as a third sector ready to rival market and state, with a quiet revolution in how your voluntary action and charitable work serves the community. (Brown, G., 2004)

The most obvious feature of this 'quiet revolution' has been the sheer growth in size of the voluntary sector over this period. According to one study, the number of charities grew by 40% in the decade from 1995 (Davies, 2006). By 2004, there were 150,000 registered charities in Britain and another 200,000 non-charitable voluntary and community organisations (cited by Brown, G., 2004). In 2006, 38% of their income was derived from statutory sources. Among them, these organisations employed 608,000 people, an increase of 45,000 since 2000 (Davies, 2006) (hence the limitations of the term 'voluntary sector').

Driving that growth is a political vision of the relationship between the state, civil society and active citizenship. The third sector is seen by New Labour as central to this vision in two main ways: first, as a provider of services; and, second, as a vehicle for strengthening civil (or civic) society through encouraging active citizenship and overcoming social exclusion. In relation to this second objective, Powell (2001, p 118) notes:

> The renewal of civil society has been associated with demands for a larger role for voluntary welfare provision in both Western society and the former Soviet Bloc. The voluntary sector is perceived as (1) an alternative to state bureaucracy and professional elitism and (2) a public space between government and the market.

Civil (or civic) society is a concept that has become fashionable over the past decade, despite, or because of, the fact that it often seems to mean all things to all people (Powell, 2001). In its most general sense, it refers to all those voluntary, community, religious and private networks and organisations that are not part of the state. Its lack of precision, however, means that it has been employed both by activists involved in the movement against neoliberal globalisation to point to a different notion of community and belonging, and also by politicians of the main political parties in the UK to evoke communitarian notions of neighbourliness and 'active citizenship'. To quote Gordon Brown once more (Brown, G., 2004):

Britain – because there is such a thing as society – as a community of communities. Tens of thousands of local neighbourhood civic associations, unions, charities, voluntary organisations. Each one unique and each one very special, not inward looking or exclusive. A Britain energised by a million centres of neighbourliness and compassion that together embody that very British idea – civic society. It is an idea that best defines a Britain that has always rejected absolutism and crude selfish individualism and always wanted to expand that space between state and markets.

It is in the creation (or re-creation, depending on perspective) of this model of Britain that the voluntary sector is seen as having a central role to play. The particular qualities and characteristics seen as equipping the sector to play this role will be considered in the next section. What is less clear, however, is how compatible these qualities are with the requirement that voluntary organisations take on a service delivery role in the context of a social care market. Paxton and his colleagues (2005, p 3) identify a dilemma arising from what they see as two potentially contradictory strands of government thinking about the role of the voluntary and community sector (VCS):

> The first strand, which focuses on reform of the state, stresses the need to fashion a more plural, democratic and responsive state to replace one which is overly centralised and bureaucratic. This approach primarily sees the VCS as a potential provider of public services. The second strand of thought is one that policy makers and politicians have rediscovered in recent years: one which emphasises the value of 'community' and 'civil renewal'. The VCS is central to most discussions of it too. On the face of it these two debates could generate contradictory implications for the relationship between the state and VCS: one driving them towards greater integration, the other emphasising separation and the distinct value of the VCS as part of civil society.

More generally, the same market forces that, as we saw in Chapter Four, have transformed local authority social work services and the experience of those who work in them over the past decade have also transformed voluntary sector organisations. The focus of the remainder of this chapter will be on the extent to which these transformations have affected the scope for radical practice within these organisations.

Promoting the third sector

What, then, are the qualities that are seen as making third sector organisations distinctive and particularly suited to the dual role outlined above? Some of these qualities were outlined by the Minister for the Third Sector, Phil Hope, in a speech in 2007. Hope identified five aspects of the voluntary sector which he saw as being of particular significance.

First, he argued, there is its closeness to the people it serves. This 'gives it a real fingertip feel for the issues that matter to its clients. It means that when local authorities are thinking about commissioning services, the third sector is likely to provide a ready-made well of expertise and knowledge about some key areas of need in their communities' (Hope, 2007).

Second, the third sector brings particular strengths to the task of service delivery: 'There's a lot of evidence that the third sector can deliver a range of services that combine innovation, precise targeting of need, measurable outcomes – and also admirable efficiency' (Hope, 2007).

Third, precisely because they are not statutory organisations, third sector organisations are seen as capable of establishing trusting relationships with people who would often avoid contact with local authority social work services or statutory mental health services: 'They are on the ground, living the reality that their clients live, dealing with the issues that their clients deal with….They have an extraordinary reach into communities which are sometimes closed to all levels of government' (Hope, 2007).

Fourth, there is their independence from the state. It is this independence that means that the third sector can 'look at problems with fresh eyes and think of solutions that don't have to take account of vested institutional interests – ideas that challenge us all to rethink traditional ways of doing things' (Hope, 2007).

Fifth, that independence, Hope argues, is also the basis of the campaigning role of voluntary sector organisations, which allows them to highlight pressing areas of need and hold public authorities to account in terms of the quality of services they deliver. In embracing the third sector, he suggests, government 'should never stifle that campaigning voice': 'Charities shouldn't have to operate in a climate of fear when they consider whether to campaign politically or not. We want them to feel confident in their role of giving voices to the voiceless, the marginalised and excluded – we wean them to be able to argue for changes to government policy and laws' (Hope, 2007).

The list of features identified by Hope as some of the strengths of the voluntary sector – its closeness to people, ability to innovate, informality, independence and scope for campaigning – is very similar to one offered more than a decade ago by Marjorie Mayo (1994) in her book *Communities and Caring: The Mixed Economy of Welfare*. In that book, however, Mayo also expressed concerns that it was precisely these characteristics of the voluntary sector that would be undermined by the changes being introduced by the recently implemented 1990 NHS and Community Care Act.

To what extent, then, do third sector organisations continue to exhibit these characteristics? Are there still spaces for workers to engage in forms of radical practice that are no longer possible within the state sector? To explore these issues, we brought together a group of experienced social workers and managers from a range of voluntary sector organisations across West and Central Scotland. These were: Laura, qualified as a social worker for 13 years, who is currently working as a practice teacher in a large national organisation; Eric, who has a nursing background and works as a service user support worker for a small mental health organisation; Doreen, qualified as a social worker for 30 years, who has spent the last 17 years working at different levels in mental health and homeless charities; Kate, who has been in social work for 17 years, during the last seven of which she has been seconded from a local authority to a large national voluntary organisation that provides social education for young people; Alice, qualified as a social worker for 26 years, who has worked mainly in voluntary sector mental health organisations but currently works in mediation; Frances, qualified as a social worker for 25 years, who has substantial experience in both the statutory and voluntary sector and is now working as a learning development manager in a national homeless charity; and George, qualified as a social worker for 22 years, who, unlike the other social workers in the group, has always worked in the voluntary sector.

Working in the third sector: potential and possibilities

A majority of these workers began their professional lives working in the local authority sector. From the discussion, it was apparent that what had persuaded several of them to move to the voluntary sector were those aspects identified in the previous section. Foremost among these was the possibility for doing relationship-based work. For most of the focus group members, the opportunities to work in this way seemed greater in voluntary sector organisations, for three main reasons. First, and most obviously, service users engaged with the service on a *voluntary* basis. In Doreen's words:

'One of the really enjoyable things in the voluntary sector is the fact that you're not the statutory sector, so people work with you voluntarily and that makes a huge difference in terms of the relationship you can build with service users.'

Where there was no prospect of a worker removing a child or contributing to a compulsory detention under mental health legislation, then one major barrier to building trust was removed.

Second, even where issues of power and control did arise, the fact that voluntary organisations were in general less subject to statutory mandates meant that it was more possible for workers to engage with service users on a more open, less procedural, basis. As Frances put it:

> 'In the voluntary sector you're able to engage with people in a much more person-centred way whereas the statutory sector are operating community care assessments which are essentially deficit-led – "Tell us everything that's wrong and why and we'll come up with a plan to fix it".'

Third, caseloads were often considerably smaller, with more time to spend with individual service users. For Kate, working for a large national voluntary organisation, she and her fellow workers were in a 'luxury position' compared with local authority staff since:

> '[T]he numbers that we work with in comparison to what somebody maybe in a team would work with, you know it's night and day, and I suppose that's the luxury of building up relationships and respect, and getting to know the service users in a totally different way from area teams.'

A fourth factor that had attracted some of these workers to voluntary sector organisations was the explicit commitment of these organisations to a value base of user empowerment. While this meant different things to different people, at bottom it meant that workers in these organisations explicitly sought to challenge both the lack of power of service users and the stigma they experienced. For Doreen this involved:

> 'Not being as far removed from service users as I certainly felt when I was a social worker and in terms of trying to involve them in more meaningful ways in the work and in the way the projects are run.'

Other focus group members provided examples of other ways in which service users were involved in their organisations. In the mental health charity in which Eric worked, for example, a policy of positive discrimination in favour of people who had experienced mental health problems was applied when filling full-time posts, while service users also sat on the Board of Management as trustees and directors. In Kate's organisation, young people and parents were involved in staff interviews (and were appropriately recompensed for doing so), something, as she noted, that would rarely, if ever, happen in statutory social work services: "I imagine social workers or teachers would freak out at the idea of being interviewed by a service user!".

A fifth attraction of some parts of the voluntary sector, particularly during the 1980s and 1990s, was the scope they seemed to offer for a more political, campaigning approach. For Alice, this had been a major factor in her decision to work in her organisation:

> 'I suppose that's why I went into the voluntary sector, that's why I made that shift ... I think it was political ... it was about gaps in services and it was about advocating on behalf of people. It was about empowerment, all these words, and that's why I went into it. That is a real strength for me, that's why I chose – against the background of salaries and all the other things – to go and work there because that was important, because it fitted with your values.'

The 'contract culture': change and constraints

If there was a large measure of agreement among this group as to what had drawn them to work in the voluntary sector in the first place, there was also consensus that the sector had changed enormously in recent years. Underpinning this change was the shift in the way in which voluntary organisations were funded, following the implementation of the 1990 NHS and Community Care Act. Whereas previously they had relied on grants from government, local authorities or other public bodies, now they were required to tender for contracts, often to these same bodies. The development of a 'contract culture' based on competition appeared to have had profound repercussions for almost every aspect of their functioning.

As noted above, for example, the possibility of developing informal relationships and spending time working with individuals was something that these focus group members particularly valued. The fact, however, that contracts now often require organisations to quantify exactly how much time workers will spend with service users on a daily or weekly basis reduces that possibility and can also lead to a 'tick box' approach. Contrasting her current situation with her early experience in the voluntary sector where she worked with a 'hard to reach' client group of homeless people with mental health problems, Doreen commented:

> 'That to me was a great experience and you could see people really, really moving on and I think it was the time you could give them that was the main factor in that. I have to say that in my last few years

in the voluntary sector that wasn't as possible and that's because the funding moved exactly from being grant funded to contracts.'

Referring specifically to the Supporting People funding on which many voluntary organisations now rely, she suggested:

'You are paid to provide so many hours' support. You no longer get paid for staff having meeting times or travel or anything else like that, you get paid for direct face-to-face support work but you only get so much per person so you therefore have to work with a much larger number of people for less hours … people are still so controlled and they had to account for every hour of what they were doing, you had to record every hour every phone call, that kind of thing, and it's really difficult to be innovative, I think, in that situation.'

Not all focus group members were ambivalent or hostile towards this new environment. Frances, for example, described it as "a tremendous opportunity", which gave the voluntary sector the chance to address previous weaknesses, including a lack of professionalism and lack of accountability:

'What the competitive environment is doing is helping to professionalise social care and from my point of view we should be able to document what we do. If we are being given budgets we should be able to manage these effectively … before we were given an awful lot of money without being accountable for the processes we put in place to do that properly.'

She also felt that service commissioners were increasingly being forced to address quality issues and to recognise that "it's more cost-effective to pay dearer to get it right first time than to do it wrong three of four times". Responding to some of the criticisms of the statutory sector, for example, Frances suggested that:

'I equally have spent more time tearing my hair out in the voluntary sector…. I had to say at times "Where's your management? What are your outcomes? What are we actually doing here to put a management structure in place that means we're all going in the same direction and we understand what we're there to achieve?". So I spent a lot of time going "Where's the procedures and policies?" and over the last 10 to 12 years that's evolved but I think we can learn from each other much more clearly.'

All focus group members agreed with Frances on the need for accountability within the sector. Some felt, however, that the constant pressure to produce reports evidencing outcomes (a pressure that seemed to them to be much greater in the voluntary sector than in the statutory sector) often got in the way of direct work with service users. Another area of concern was the impact of competition in the sector on staff conditions. Some commentators have referred to a 'race to the bottom' within the voluntary sector and that view seemed to be reflected in the comments of some other members, for example, Doreen:

> 'My experience has been that workers' conditions have gone down and down and down, the wages have gone down, the hours have gone up.... We started working thirty-seven-and-a-half hours instead of thirty-five hours a week and the staff accepted it. We didn't get our annual increments. So that is how they managed to stay in business.... There is something about being professional in an organisation but how on earth do you provide empowering practice if workers are totally disempowered? I don't think it's possible.'

Laura, from the perspective of a national, well-established charity, also expressed concern about the ways in which competition was affecting staff wages and conditions:

> 'Our organisation's very much getting into competing with the private sector. To do that, we're creating a new grade of staff which is lower than a support worker, it's a support assistant who gets paid not very much money but also I've got a feeling that they don't actually have to do SVQ [Scottish Vocational Qualification] stuff, which support workers have to do, so again, that's not very professional.'

Focus group members also drew attention to the ways in which inequality in size and resources affected organisations' ability to compete effectively. Doreen again:

> 'The organisations who win the contracts are the big organisations because they have got professional people to make the applications, whereas in smaller organisations it's down to the project managers or whoever happens to be around.'

Kate, working in one of the largest and wealthiest children's charities, provided a striking example of what such inequalities can mean in practice:

'We've just changed our logo, which means every service as well as the organisation has changed letterheads, campaigning and stuff like that and probably what the organisation has spent on that alone would have paid for one or two of the smaller organisations' funding for a year or whatever.'

The competition, of course, is not solely between voluntary organisations. As George pointed out:

'One of the other problems is that it's not a level playing field between local authorities and the voluntary sector and budgets are tight and voluntary sector agencies are getting cut rather than the local authority.'

Competition, in the social care market, as in any other market, leads to concentration and the dominance of a small number of large organisations, a phenomenon that has been noted by other analysts of the third sector:

By emphasising the importance of 'professionalism' and 'economic rationality' rather than a traditional volunteering ethos, Labour's approach to the third sector is contributing to an increasing division between grassroots voluntary groups and 'a new breed of professionalized, well-funded and well-organized voluntary organisations'. (Morison, 2000, p 103; Fyfe, 2005, p 552)

All respondents saw the disappearance of diversity, in the sense of smaller organisations being unable to survive, as a serious loss to service users. The irony of a process that is supposedly about creating 'choice' for service users but results in less choice was noted by Alice. Referring to a situation in one small town where most of the services are now provided by one large national charity, she asked:

'If people access a service and it doesn't work out and they're asked not to use that service any more, are they excluded from all services? So I think there's stuff around choice for people.'

Faced with this situation, some respondents felt that organisations were left with essentially two options: either to opt out of service provision altogether and continue to play a traditional campaigning/advocacy role or to find other ways of competing effectively in this new marketplace. The mental health charity to which Eric belonged had gone for the first option. He felt that there were both advantages and disadvantages in this:

'You keep the flexibility, you keep light on your feet but to a degree, you rely almost on the crumbs from the table, you know. The other side of that is if you decide to go into providing care and core services, you become almost a part of the system and you're governed by your contracts and your service-level agreements.... You almost have to grow to succeed and you lose the personal and local touch.'

Others were split on the extent to which the other option, of engaging in effective competition to provide services while holding on to social work values, providing high-quality services *and* ensuring good conditions for staff, was a viable one. Kate felt that the large national organisation to which she belonged had the capacity to do this, while acknowledging that wage levels there were still far lower than in the local authority. George felt that, alongside the competition, there was still scope for collaboration and that by entering into partnerships, even small organisations could hold their own. Others felt that organisations could survive if they were able to develop a 'niche market' and develop expertise in the skills of effective competition. In that sense, all of the organisations to which these focus group members belonged were actively trying to find ways of competing without losing sight of a model of provision that valued both service users and staff. What was less clear, though, was how far this new competitive environment continued to allow them to develop the relationship-based work, service user empowerment and campaigning strategies that, as we saw earlier, were the things that had brought them into these organisations in the first place.

More losers than winners?

Box 5.3: One worker's experience

The following quote comes from a person who works at a refugee charity delivering a contract on behalf of the Legal Services Commission (LSC). The charity provides advice and representation to asylum seekers and immigrants:

We have had annual pay increases ad infinitum but this year they told us because of the budget situation they couldn't afford a pay increase at all. There might be a bonus if we hit the target. But because we are adrift of our target there's no chance of that.

> There's a long-hours culture and there are serious problems relating to that. In order to meet the targets people are working 40 or 50 hours. It's very pressured. The LSC are changing the contract in 2009 which, overnight, is going to wipe out one third of our funding. They are moving from an hourly rate to a fixed fee in each case, regardless of how many hours you do. It's going to mean redundancies; it can't mean anything else. LSC is going to competitive tendering in the future and we know what that means: it's the lowest price, and it doesn't matter what's provided. (Little, 2008)

As this example suggests, the experience of the Scottish workers in the previous section is far from being unusual. *False Economy?*, a study carried out by academics at Strathclyde University and Oxford Brookes University (Cunningham and James, 2007), explored the impact of the contract culture on 12 voluntary organisations across the UK. The study found:

- There is an intensifying climate of competition and anxiety among workers and their representatives regarding future employment prospects.
- Workers in these organisations could be subject to all aspects of employment insecurity but the threat of job loss and changes to terms and conditions were the most acute.
- There is work intensification across the sector stemming from a combination of worsening staff–client ratios, changing user needs and increased administrative work.
- Small voluntary organisations are more exposed than larger ones to the threat of detrimental changes to terms and conditions. Indeed, the majority of smaller organisations appeared to face significant threats to their survival in the current climate.
- Views regarding the impact of the insecure funding environment on quality of care were mixed but the majority of management, activist and worker interviews revealed significant concerns.

Finally the aspects of the insecure contracting environment that most affected service quality were found to be:

- greater demands on management time and resources;
- heightened bureaucracy associated with programmes such as Supporting People;
- reduced staffing levels;
- threats to continuity of care from employee turnover and falls in employee morale.

While the main focus of this study was on the impact of the contract culture on workers' conditions, its authors also explored some of the ways in which these changes affected the quality of the service provided. A major concern here was the way in which the increased bureaucracy associated with funding streams like Supporting People and the need for organisations on short-term funding (the majority) always to be chasing their next contract reduced their time to spend with service users: 'It's looking, constantly looking and searching for modes of funding and that is what is time consuming. We will go anywhere' (Cunningham and James, 2007, p 18).

That lack of time also affected the capacity of workers and managers to think and act strategically and led to a more reactive approach. A worker from a small advisory service commented:

> It's the added value bit ... it's not well connected or as joined up as it should be. Let's say there is a lot of stuff we could be doing. We are very reactive, but there is more work we could be doing with councils and social landlords to prevent the problems arising in the first place. We are not spending enough time on that and that is what you should be doing but we don't and we don't have enough time. (Cunningham and James, 2007, p 18)

Finally, the study found that workers in the last few months were reluctant to take on new cases, as they did not feel they would be able to offer an ongoing service:

> You have to get the balance right between being able to commit ... and thinking in the back of your mind, am I actually going to be here in six months and is there someone to take this over and pass this onto. You know it's really difficult because you don't want to let the person down. (Cunningham and James, 2007, p 21)

Given the importance that the focus group members in our study attached to relationship-based work, the loss of opportunities for such work implicit in the above statement, and for continuity of care more generally, suggests that the contract culture has had a negative impact on this aspect of quality of care.

Perhaps not surprisingly, given the pressures on staff discussed earlier, recent years have seen a considerable rise in industrial unrest within the voluntary sector. Thus, in April 2007, staff at the Scottish care organisation, Quarriers, took strike action over pay. In the same year, a strike was narrowly averted at a learning disabilities charity, the Elfrida Society, by a last-minute pay offer. In February 2008, 450 staff from the housing charity, Shelter, also took strike action, following the introduction of a new employment contract that proposed to add half an hour to the working day and to end yearly pay increases (*Guardian Society*, Charities section, 20 February 2008).

Growing the private sector

Finally, we shall consider the role now played by the private sector in the provision of social work and social care. As noted earlier, terms such as the 'independent sector' or the 'third sector' tend to elide what had previously been seen as a fundamental divide within welfare provision. On one side of this divide were services provided by local authority or voluntary sector organisations, operating on a not-for-profit basis; on the other were those provided by private organisations required to make a profit if they are to remain in business. Reinforcing this distinction was the widely held welfare state principle that access to social services, whether provided by the state or the voluntary sector, should be based on need, not ability to pay, and that the profit motive had no place in addressing the needs of poor and vulnerable clients. In the words of the leading theorist of the early welfare state, 'There are some services which, with strong public support, government have recognised as being intrinsically suited to organization on the welfare principle, as public, non-profit, non-commercial services, available to all on a uniform standard irrespective of means' (Marshall, 1981, p 134).

Against that background, the use of terms such as the 'independent sector' by successive UK governments committed to neoliberal policies can be seen as an attempt to blur that distinction and to legitimise the role of the private sector in welfare provision, usually under the banner of 'increasing choice'. This section will assess how successful they have been in this endeavour, looking first at residential social care and home care, then at professional social work.

Residential social care

The most significant transfer of services from the public to the private sector has taken place in the area of residential social care. Thus, by the end of the 1990s, only 22% of the residential care market remained in the public sector (for the UK as a whole), compared with 63% in 1970 and 39% in 1990. Across the whole range of care accommodation, 81% of residents were in 'independent' facilities compared with 61% in 1990 (Knapp et al, 2001, p 289; see also Carey, 2008). A similar trend has occurred in childcare (Carey, 2008, p 921). Politicians and academics committed to 'Third Way' perspectives frequently argue that such a shift should not concern us since what matters is not who provides the care but rather the quality of care provided. Even leaving aside, however, wider issues about the place of profit-making businesses in meeting people's basic needs, the evidence does not support the view that the involvement of the private sector has increased the quality of care in this area.

First, in terms of increased choice, in practice a very small number of multinational companies, such as BUPA and Four Seasons Health Care, now dominate the sector. Whereas the care home market in the 1980s was characterised by a large number of small proprietors, by January 2000 just 18 large companies operated roughly 1,360 homes, 22% of all private sector UK provision (Knapp et al, 2001, p 292). Arguably, therefore, there is now *less* choice for those entering residential care. Second, in terms of the quality of care provided, by 2001 the size of the average care home had grown from an average of 19 beds to 30 beds, despite the fact that smaller units are generally regarded as offering scope for more individualised provision (Pollock, 2004, pp 18-19). A third factor affecting quality of care is the poor pay and conditions of the staff who work in them (Davies, 2006). Finally, continuity of care is usually regarded as a core element of good-quality care for older people especially. However, the combination of high staff turnover on the one hand and a high rate of home closure on the other (800 a year between 2000 and 2003; according to Pollock, 2004, p 190) make this less rather than more likely to be achieved in private care settings.

Home care

The picture in home care (or domiciliary care, as it was called previously) is very similar. Scourfield (2007) illustrates that, in 1992, only 2% of domiciliary care was provided by private sector providers; by 2000, this had risen to 56%, a trend that seems likely to continue. Driving this shift is the contracting out of staff and services by a majority of local councils. According to the Commission for Social Care Inspection for England and Wales in its 2007 Annual Report (CSCI, 2007a), the demand for private social care including help with cleaning, medication, bathing, shopping and other support has risen rapidly in England and Wales as cash-strapped councils have restricted help to older and disabled people (the situation in Scotland is different, following the Scottish Executive's decision in 2002 to provide free personal care). The report noted, however, that the quality of private care was 'patchy', with people paying for care having to face a 'cottage industry' of providers, many of them small and inexperienced, paying low wages to poorly qualified employees and with high rates of staff turnover. While most treated people with dignity, 'a substantial number of home care services are failing standards relating to medication, recruitment and selection of staff, and supervision' (CSCI, 2007a, p 10). Families and individuals, the report continued, increasingly have to take the strain as social services departments restrict the service they provide to people with 'substantial' or 'critical' needs:

> Councils are tightening the rules about who qualifies for state-funded social care. More and more older and disabled people either have to find and pay for their own private care or rely on family members or friends.... Informal carers have to fill in the gaps, with inadequate support structures and no system in many areas to help people find the services they need. (CSCI, 2007b)

The result is that 'The options for people who do not meet the criteria set by their local council are limited.... In some cases people rely on friends and family members. In others they pay for their own care. Some people have no option but to do without' (CSCI, 2007b).

Private social work

Compared with the enormous expansion of the private sector that has taken place in the residential and home care sectors over the past decade, private practice still makes up a very small part of professional social work practice in the UK. According to one workforce survey published in 2005, 71% of social workers are employed by local councils, a further 17% by other public bodies and voluntary organisations, 7% by the private sector and 4% by agencies (Skills for Care, 2005). Nevertheless, private social work practice has made some inroads into British social work. There is now, for example, a Professional Association for Family Court Advisers and Independent Social Work Practitioners (NAGALRO), which has set up a directory for those wishing to commission an independent social worker. The British Association of Social Workers (BASW) has set up a similar directory and in addition has created an Independents' Forum with 380 consultants on its books in 2005 (out of a total BASW membership of 10,000).

One of the few pieces of research into the growth of private social work practice has looked at the experience in New Zealand, where, as in Britain, neoliberal welfare policies were vigorously promoted by governments during the 1980s and 1990s (Heugten and Daniels, 2001). Researchers there found that, as with the voluntary sector workers whose views were discussed in this chapter, organisational discontent was a major 'push' factor in persuading workers to move out of local authority employment. They report that by 1994, for example, the New Zealand Children and Young Persons Service had undergone nine restructurings in as many years while the public hospital system where mental health social workers were based had been similarly reshaped: 'Many social workers and other public welfare workers had become disillusioned and "burnt out" during this time. Restructuring was the most prevalent reason cited by respondents for leaving organised employment to enter private practice' (Heugten and Daniels, 2001, p 745).

A number of other factors, however, were also important. Thus, in both New Zealand and the UK, the constant disparagement by government and media throughout the 1980s and 1990s of social work as a 'failing profession', against a background mantra of 'public bad, private good', probably helped some workers overcome their initial reservations about moving into private practice. Referring to the impact of 'Rogernomics', for example (the New Zealand version of Reaganomics and Thatcherism), one respondent commented:

> I think that's had an influence on me too, you know, the kind of political and ideological shift that's occurred in the '90's and the late '80's in New Zealand. It's almost like – I don't agree with it but it seems like the message has come through with the advent of Rogernomics – it's okay to be greedy, it's okay to go for yourself and go for what you want and to hell with the rest of them, the bloke next to me, whatever. (cited in Heugten and Daniels, 2001, p 746)

No less important in both countries, however, has been a policy context that emphasises 'choice' of providers and which encourages and promotes the role of the private sector in the delivery of public services, including social work services. One proposal of the 2007 Green Paper for England and Wales *Care Matters: Transforming the Lives of Children and Young People in Care* (DCSF, 2007), for example, was to explore 'the feasibility of piloting new independent "social care practices", small independent groups of workers who contract with the local authority to provide services to children in care' (DCSF, 2007, p 7).

Given such official encouragement, it is not surprising that 'independent' social workers should now feel that their time has come. For one enthusiast, 'A recent increase in the number of highly skilled and experienced independent children and family social workers should be seen as a major opportunity for social work to re-affirm itself as a strong and autonomous profession' (Willis, 2007). In fact, however, there are some very good reasons why this trend should be resisted.

First, there are the ethical objections. As late as 1979, BASW considered private social work practice 'unethical'. In the most recent edition of *Case Critical*, a classic text of Canadian radical social work, Carniol (2005) shows why these objections still hold. To remain in business, such practitioners need to make a profit, which means they must charge a fee for their services. As

Carniol (2005, p 109) notes, in practice this means working with people who can afford to pay – 'a middle-class clientele. In exchange for payment, such clients receive counselling on how better to cope with psychological tensions, work pressures, and personal troubles'. As with private medicine, those who cannot afford to pay – in reality the majority of people who use social work services – are excluded. It is difficult to see how this is compatible with basic notions of anti-oppressive practice. Alternatively, these practitioners may choose to work on an independent basis for solicitors or, more commonly, local authorities, in family court work for example. Here too, the scope for a critical or anti-oppressive approach is severely constrained. As Carniol (2005, p 109) comments, on the basis of the Canadian experience:

> When social workers carry out such contracts for a state agency, they have come full circle in collaborating with the state. True, they have won a measure of independence in their day-to-day work: they are no longer civil servants. But when they receive government contracts, they are expected to carry out work that does not question the constraints or type of service allowed by these contracts.

A second set of objections to private social work practice concerns its impact on social work more generally, and on critical or radical approaches in particular. In most of the countries where it is practised (including Canada, New Zealand and the US), much, if not most, private practice takes the form of individual counselling and psychotherapy. As Heugten and Daniels (2001, p 740) note, the creation of a market for such services rests on a concept of 'personal problems' and a belief that these can be resolved on a personal, intra-psychic basis rather than requiring structural change. In practice this means both a considerable reduction in the range of social work methods employed (with community development and social action approaches the main losers) and a narrowing, if not abandonment, of notions of anti-oppressive practice that link 'personal problems' to 'public issues', in the sense of addressing the discrimination and oppression that mar the lives of so many clients.

Finally, a growth in private practice is likely to increase, rather than reduce, the bureaucracy and managerialism that frustrate and demoralise so many local authority practitioners. According to Willis (2007) in his defence of private practice, 'The advantage for local authorities of commissioning out discrete pieces of work to independent social workers – so-called spot purchasing – is that it frees up council social workers who juggle with a huge array of functions at the area office, many of which keep them away from front-line services'. The argument is a spurious one for two reasons. First, as Dustin (2007) has shown in her book *The McDonaldization of Social Work*, much of the 'huge array of functions' that practitioners currently experience flows directly from the introduction of care management approaches in the early 1990s, in the context of a social care market. Private practice is a product and symptom of that process, not a solution. Second, creaming off the more lucrative – and often more prestigious – areas of work to private practitioners will further downgrade the status of local authority social work and reinforce the 'image of the independent social work practitioner ... as a confident, self-reliant and skilled individual' (Willis, 2007) at the expense of area team workers who are often doing equally skilled work but under far more difficult circumstances.

Conclusion: nowhere to run

If there is one single conclusion emerging from this chapter, it is that the traditional image of the voluntary sector, as a refuge from the bureaucracy and managerialism of local authority social work, a place where 'real' social work can be practised, is increasingly hard to sustain. This is most apparent in the face of inadequate short-term funding, underpaid and often under-trained staff, and, at best, patchy levels of service user involvement. None of this, of course, will prevent both of the main political parties in the UK from continuing to present the sector as being 'innovative, efficient and effective' (Labour Party, 2005, p 105). The creation by government in 2006 of an Office for the Third Sector reflects the increased role it envisages for voluntary and private organisations in the delivery of welfare services and more especially in the latest phase of welfare reform, which is concerned with getting more disabled people back into the workforce (Freud, 2007; Black, 2008). In this situation, a three-pronged response is necessary.

First, at a national level, workers should support campaigns that seek to improve the funding of the sector, including minimum five-year contracts for service providers and proper funding to provide secure jobs for workers (and consequently greater continuity of care for service users). The Fair Funding for Voluntary Sector Services statement issued by the Scottish Convention for Voluntary Organisations and several leading trade unions in 2007 goes some way towards addressing these issues (SCVO, 2007).

Second, progressive practice with service users, whether in the state sector or the voluntary sector, is only possible on the basis of decent working conditions, including workloads that allow time to be spent with service users, training opportunities, reasonable levels of pay and security of employment. As discussed above, growing numbers of voluntary sector trade unionists have been involved in industrial action in recent years in an attempt to defend these very basic conditions. Whatever the practical difficulties, there is still no substitute for building strong trade union organisation within the voluntary sector.

Finally, as this chapter and the previous chapter have shown, good social work practice in both the state sector and the voluntary sector is being undermined by the very same processes of marketisation and managerialism. Creating new forums at local level (for example, seminars, social work action networks or union-based issue groups) and also at national level (such as the Social Work: A Profession Worth Fighting For? conference series, which will be discussed in the final chapter) is crucial, as a means both of overcoming divisions among groups of social workers and of sharing experiences of resistance and of good practice.

Questions for discussion

- ⊃ Think of voluntary organisations with which you have had contact. To what extent do they exhibit the qualities suggested by Minister for the Third Sector, Phil Hope, in the discussion in this chapter?
- ⊃ What strengths or advantages might the local authority social work sector have as compared with voluntary organisations?
- ⊃ Some critics have described the expansion of the voluntary sector as involving a form of 'soft privatisation'. Do you agree?

Suggestions for further reading

- ⊃ Charities Commission (2007) *Stand and Deliver: The Future for Charities Delivering Public Services*, London: Charities Commission. Based on a consultation with almost 4,000 charities, a useful overview of the scale and impact of charities on public service delivery.
- ⊃ Davies, S. (2007) *Third Sector Provision of Local Government and Health Services*, London: UNISON; Cunningham, I. and James, P. (2007) *False Economy? The Costs of Contracting and Workforce Insecurity in the Voluntary Sector*, London: UNISON. Two reports by academics commissioned by the public sector union UNISON, which provide a detailed, critical analysis of the impact of the 'contract culture' on public sector provision.

⮑   IRISS (Institute for Research and Innovation in Social Services) (2008) *The Golden Bridge: Child Migration from Scotland to Canada 1869-1939*, online exhibition, Dundee: IRISS, www.iriss.ac.uk/goldenbridge. A powerful and moving exploration of the experience of the 7,000 'home children' who migrated to Canada from Quarriers' Homes in Scotland.

⮑   Lavalette, M. and Ferguson, I. (2007) 'Democratic language and neoliberal practice: the problem with civil society', *International Social Work*, 50 (4), pp 447-59. A critical discussion of the concept of civil society with a specific focus on the role of voluntary and non-governmental organisations in the provision of social care, both in Britain and internationally.

6

Beyond good intentions: the challenge from service users and carers

Introduction

Louise's story reflects the current experiences of many adults with learning disabilities. In various ways, life for Louise is much improved since the disagreeable days of 'the hospital'. She has a comfortable and safe house to live in, companionship, support and some control over her own affairs. At the same time, though, she remains more dependent on others than she needs to be, the services she receives are under-resourced and inconsistent and she has little opportunity to effect change beyond small alterations to daily routines.

The user involvement agenda in the UK is an enormously complex matter. For a start, few seem agreed about the terminology: is it user and carer involvement, empowerment, participation or leadership? In addition, despite a strong policy emphasis on involvement, there is little evidence to suggest that developments have, as Louise's circumstances serve to illustrate, produced meaningful results across the board for service users and carers (Beresford, 2007).

As we saw in Chapters Four and Five, practitioners sometimes struggle, for a variety of reasons, to remain connected to service users in constructive ways, especially in the state sector. Broadly, though, social workers are accepting of service user and carer participation, and many welcome it. User and carer involvement in social services is a multifaceted concept, however; one characterised by ambiguity, apprehension and tension, riddled with misconceptions about how power is used and experienced and associated with politically imposed ideas of individualisation and consumerism that are often difficult to embrace. However, related, as it also is, to notions of citizenship and empowerment, user involvement means that social work managers and practitioners have, in many cases, had to rethink their attitudes to, and relationships with, service users. We welcome a challenge to the assumption that social workers, together with health professionals, are the experts in service users' or patients' problems. In keeping with Cowden and Singh (2007, p 5), though, while acknowledging that 'user knows best', we suggest that all too often developments in user involvement are made to sound and look good but lack substance and have little impact. What we shall argue here is that it takes a true commitment to critical and radical practice and management before social work can genuinely move forward with and for service users and carers.

This chapter will discuss briefly the historical background to user involvement. Although a critical perspective will be taken, it is our belief that authentic user involvement is a crucial aspect of radical social work. This is because of the extent to which it is service users and carers who have, in recent years, offered creative challenges to professional power and influence. The chapter will then explore aspects of service user and carer participation that can be viewed as potentially radical, for example, full information-giving and active listening, discussion and consultation, involvement in steering groups and management committees, support and advocacy and campaigning. In particular, the disability movement and the mental health users' movement will be considered, as these have proved to be most influential. Indeed, both of these movements are strongly represented on the Stirling University Social Work User and Carer Involvement Group, whose members helped us enormously with this book by taking part in regular meetings at university and contributing to a focus group discussion. Attention will also be paid to children and young people and to people who offend, in recognition that their voices tend to be marginalised in the user involvement arena.

The politics behind the involvement agenda

Driving the user involvement agenda forward in the UK now is government policy, specifically the New Labour modernisation programme (Harris, 2003; Scourfield, 2007). This is not to suggest that service user participation was not a political hot potato before New Labour came to power; it was, and for several reasons. As Cowden and Singh's (2007) summary of user involvement's history suggests, and as was noted in previous chapters here, social work, and other professions, came under pressure during the 1970s from new social movements. Feminist, anti-racist and gay and lesbian rights movements added their voices to those of the 'old' social movements like socialism and trade unionism:

> Throughout the 1970s … we begin to see a disjuncture emerging between, on the one hand, professionals and non-professionals (citizens, clients, users, activists etc) and on the other assumptions about the kind of society Britain was becoming … the emergence of New Social Movements [was] a sure sign that the assumptions that had underpinned the post-war world were coming unstuck. (Cowden and Singh, 2007, p 8)

Change was coming to social work anyway as these new discourses around power and professionalism began to filter through to policy and practice. Other new social movements had particular resonance for social work throughout the 1970s, 1980s and 1990s, however. In particular, the disability movement (Campbell, 1997) and the mental health users' movement (Barnes and Shardlow, 1996; Crossley, 1999) raised concrete concerns about how far removed the social work and medical professions were from those they were supposed to be helping and supporting. That some service user groups were beginning to challenge the way in which society in general, and service providers in particular, viewed them encouraged a fairly radical rethink of identity, labelling, stigma and power. As discussed in Chapter Three, however, change was also coming to social work throughout the 1980s and 1990s as major ideological shifts occurred in the UK in the name of neoliberalism.

The arrival of Thatcherite neoliberalism saw the beginnings of the modernisation process by which the relationship between the citizen and the state was reconstructed (Scourfield, 2007). In terms of user involvement, the political process kicked off in 1980, when the then Conservative government commissioned an independent review of social workers' role and tasks. The report of the review process, the Barclay Report (Barclay, 1982), concluded that the original social work reforms of the 1960s had not led to accessible services or given service users much of a say. As a result, it was argued that social services needed to be more 'decentralised, generic and participatory' (Beresford, 2007, p 14); a 'community social work approach' was required (Glasby, 2005, p 66). Alongside this recommendation, Barclay also argued for informal caring to be recognised and strengthened (Glasby, 2005). Although this raised fears about the impact on women, as traditionally the main carers, and the effects on people in need who could find themselves more, rather than less, dependent on their families (Beresford, 2007), politicians remained committed to decentralisation and 'greater choice and independence' for service users (Glasby, 2005, p 69).

Little seemed to happen on the back of the Barclay Report, however, and a second review was commissioned a few years later. The recommendations of this second review, published as the Griffiths Report (Griffiths, 1988), were similar to Barclay's: increased choice, independence and involvement in services for users and carers. This time, though, legislative reform followed. In 1990, the NHS and Community Care Act was introduced and with it came a sea-change in the way in which adult services were provided in the UK. In particular, the Act emphasised 'care in the community', which opened the door to the purchaser–provider spit in services and, therefore, to privatisation and managerialism (Glasby, 2005). Indeed, the main priorities apparent in the Act were further rolling back of the welfare state and greater opportunity for financial control in the public sector. Any increased involvement or participation for service users and carers would come almost as a by-product.

As Cowden and Singh (2007, p 12) argue, community care:

> became a term that could float semiotically free, meaning something to everyone, with its vaguely progressive aura never needing to be defined concretely. Hence the triumph of the ... Act ... concerned the development of a model that was able to ... appropriate progressive demands for democratization of services, at the same

time as presenting market efficiency and the private sector as the vehicles that would deliver this.

Service users as consumers

As documented in Chapters Three and Four, from the 1980s onwards, social work has come under extreme pressure from the twin forces of marketisation and managerialism. A third aspect of the neoliberal agenda, however, is consumerism (Harris, 2003), which aims to 'transform the passive social services "client" into a discriminating "consumer"' (Scourfield, 2007, p 108) by emphasising the right to 'freedom' and 'choice' (McLaughlin, H., 2008). The shift from 'client' to 'consumer', however, is problematic for several reasons. First, it minimises the extent to which service users actually have choice about their contact with social work or health agencies, due, for example, to their particular needs or life circumstances (Forbes and Sashidharan, 1997). Second, it glosses over the powerful, compulsory aspects of the social work role in terms of work with people who offend, have mental health needs or struggle to provide adequate care for their children (Hodge, 2005). Third, it sidelines the extent to which government and professionals remain in control of the user involvement agenda. Most initiatives are 'top-down', rather than 'bottom-up' and, despite the growing influence of user movements (see Box 6.2), the language of user involvement is associated more with individual empowerment and responsibility than it is with social change and social justice (Ferguson, 2008). Fourth, in emphasising individual responsibility, it implies that the playing field is a level one. In so doing, it disregards structural inequality along the lines of social class, age, gender, ability, race and culture (Forbes and Sashidharan, 1997) and assumes a uniformity of rationale and ability that is just not there (McLaughlin, H., 2008).

Box 6.2: Developments in the user and carer movement

User and carer movements continue to develop in the UK. There are now strong and active groups providing support to, as well as fighting for and with, people who have mental health needs, people with learning disabilities and children looked after by the state. Moreover, the national users' network, 'Shaping Our Lives', strives to link local networks of user-controlled organisations to provide users with a more powerful voice. Scotland also has a national users' network, 'Scottish Voices', which aims to assist users and carers to influence social work education. Carers too now have dedicated local and national organisations to provide information, advice, support and advocacy.

Some useful websites
The Hearing Voices Network – www.hearing-voices.org
People First – www.peoplefirstscotland.com
The Who Cares? Trust – www.thewhocarestrust.org.uk
Shaping our Lives – www.shapingourlives.org.uk
Scottish Voices – www.iriss.ac.uk/scottishvoices
The Princess Royal Trust for Carers – www.carers.org
Crossroads (Caring for Carers) – www.crossroads.org.uk

'We are all individuals and we are all responsible'

Scourfield (2007) argues that individualised approaches gained even more momentum under New Labour in the UK. For example, direct payments, introduced at the tail end of Conservative governance in 1996, have taken off under New Labour. The idea is that direct payments emphasise 'independence and individual choice' (Scourfield, 2007, p 17) because they give individuals money to buy their own care services. As Scourfield suggests, disabled activist groups fought for direct payments, seeing them as a way in which to gain control of their lives. Early indications are that direct payments do, at times, increase service user satisfaction. Without suitable services to buy in, however, making cash available is unlikely to meet service users' needs. This was illustrated well by the service user, Kate, in her 2007 contribution to social work teaching at Stirling University that we discussed in Chapter Four. Kate explained that she had been offered direct payments to purchase services for her son (an escort and befriender) but had then been told that no such suitably trained people were available in her part of rural Scotland. Similarly, consultation with service users undertaken by the national user network 'Shaping our Lives' (Beresford, 2007), found that direct payments received insufficient funding and provided few opportunities for users to control them.

New Labour has also been the architect of the most recent development associated with consumerist ideals, 'personalisation', which purports to place users at the centre of service design and delivery. While a full discussion of personalisation and its implications is beyond the scope of this book (see Ferguson, 2007, for a detailed critique), a brief summary is in order. Personalisation ideas appeared only very recently in relation to public services (Leadbetter, 2004; Leadbetter and Lownsborough, 2005) yet are promoted as bridging the gap between paternalism and consumerism. As well as having easier access to services, and more say in the way services are delivered to them, through direct payments, for example, under personalisation models, service users become 'co-designers' and 'co-producers' of services. As the 'participation, knowledge and responsibility' of service users increase (Leadbetter, 2004, p 24), so society as a whole benefits.

Few would dispute the likely benefits to be gained by service users participating in service design and evaluation and increasing their knowledge. As Scourfield (2007, p 117) questions, however, as he debates the limitations of individualisation and responsibilisation, 'perhaps too much is expected of what even the most enterprising citizen can achieve and be responsible for'. Overemphasising the importance of individuality and responsibility just does not reflect the reality of service users' situations. With lives often blighted by poverty, inequality, oppression and stigma, the reality remains that service users have very limited choices (Forbes and Sashidharan, 1997): 'Through no fault of their own, the average social work client will often not be the "choosing", "deciding", "shaping" author of his or her own life' (Ferguson, 2008, p 80).

Box 6.3: Practice discussion – service user as consumer

Margaret, aged 31, is a lone parent of three children aged between five and 12. Margaret struggles to cope with the children at times, linked mainly to a long-term problem with heroin and the heroin substitute, methadone. Currently, the two youngest children are living with foster carers and the oldest is with her maternal grandmother. They were placed with alternative carers three weeks ago when Margaret, having taken large quantities of drugs and alcohol, became very distressed and volatile, threatening to kill herself and the children. Police and social workers became involved quickly and the children were removed from Margaret's care on an emergency basis.

Three weeks after this 'episode', Margaret is desperate to have the children back home; the children too insist that they wish to be with their mother. The periods when alternative care is required are becoming more frequent, however, because Margaret would seem to be losing control over her drug and alcohol intake and to be experiencing deteriorating physical and mental health. Social workers are concerned about the instability and disruption the children are facing and are insisting on a 'full assessment' of the family situation before any decisions are made to return the children to Margaret's care.

Questions for discussion
- What aspects of Margaret's life make it difficult for her to be independent and to exercise choice?
- What choices do Margaret's children have?

■ What can social workers do to increase the choices that Margaret has and to promote her rights?

■ As someone who uses drugs, does Margaret have the same rights and choices as other service users?

Reviewing the situation: the good, the bad and the indifferent

We offer this brief consideration of user involvement not to undermine it but to illustrate its contradictory nature and to introduce ways forward. Questions do need to be asked about the extent to which the empowerment of marginalised and stigmatised service users can truly be at the heart of a politically driven campaign that also concerns itself with economy, efficiency and effectiveness, the 'three Es' (McLaughlin, H., 2008, p 3), and with restructuring public services (Scourfield, 2007). Equally, there are doubts about the extent to which users have benefited from the surfeit of participation initiatives. As Beresford (2007) notes, user involvement goes hand in hand with notions of anti-oppressive practice, empowerment, partnership and inclusion, all of which have been incorporated into the professional social work value base. Despite these shifts, the service users' voices heard in Beresford's (2007) report still highlight much that is wrong with social work policy and service provision:

> [S]ocial work roles and tasks with both adults and children and families can be seen to be arbitrarily constrained by managerial structures, increasing bureaucratisation and funding priorities, resulting in the standardizing of social work responses and referral to a limited range of support services. (Beresford, 2007, p 48)

Users may be more involved in decision-making processes now, and may be asked more often than before what they find helpful or less helpful about social work services. Service user benefits are not an automatic consequence of user participation, however. As the above quote suggests, this is due, in part, to the shift towards managerial control in social work and the uncertainty that now surrounds the social worker's relationship with service users (Cowden and Singh, 2007). Also, as McLaughlin (2008, p 7) suggests, the *process* of involving service users now seems more important than any attempt to improve the services they receive; it is often tokenistic, something we have to be seen to do rather than something that we truly value. Taking social work education as one more example, user and carer involvement has been on the agenda for several years (Levin, 2004) but, at least in Scotland, money to support a participation programme was only just made available in

2008. For some years now we have at Stirling University encouraged service users and carers to contribute to the education of student social workers. We have, with the support of our User and Carer Involvement Group, altered aspects of our selection procedures, introduced user and carer involvement to the assessment of students' practice learning performances and developed several modules to reflect user and carer perspectives. The lack of financial support has been an enormous hindrance, however, and a problem shared with our colleagues at other Scottish universities until recently.

Another difficulty has been the perceived disjuncture between social work education and practice, with students sometimes feeling that what they are taught at university does not necessarily equip them for life in a mechanised and standardised practice arena. Lymbery and Butler (2004), in their edited text, explore ways in which practitioners can begin to bridge the gap between the ideals that brought them into the profession and the realities of practice that they face on qualification. There remains a concern, though, that user involvement is just one more hurdle for stressed-out workers to negotiate. In such a climate, tokenistic approaches might be the best that can be achieved.

The user involvement agenda is one that is worth fighting for, however. Without the mental health survivors' movement, perhaps we would still have a system that coercively confines people with serious mental health needs to psychiatric hospital, with no attempt to gain their views or those of an independent representative. Similarly, without the self-advocacy movement for people with learning disabilities, perhaps disabled men and women would still be treated in paternalistic and sometimes punitive ways in large institutions. On the back of service user and patient movements, social work has been able to embrace some of the progressive ideas about participation and empowerment that could otherwise have become trapped within academic journals. This process was helped in no small way by radical social workers and commentators of the 1970s and 1980s who first aligned themselves with the struggles of oppressed clients.

Some service users will always be less sympathetic than others, however. For example, the current publicity surrounding people who offend is more about the need for tougher enforcement of community penalties (Hedderman and Hough, 2004), and extra prisons to both punish and contain them, than it is about their often overwhelming needs. Although professionals working with people who offend often recognise the complexity of their personal and social situations and do their best to provide needs-based, as well as offence-focused, services, the pressure to 'get tough' on offenders is difficult to resist. Furthermore, there seems to be less evidence that user involvement, and associated notions of empowerment and inclusion, are doing much to improve the lot of children. The voices of children and young people will always be less powerful, and their choices more limited, than those of the adults around them. This is especially the case where children are deemed troublesome and their anti-social activities are highlighted as much as their multiple needs are disregarded (Goldson and Muncie, 2006).

As Beresford (2007) suggests, however, it is service users and carers who consistently come up with creative ideas for taking social work forward in the best interests of users and workers. What users request are services that are genuinely inclusive, participative and rights based (Beresford, 2007, p 49). This would require, for example, a willingness: to reappraise the extent to which social work is social control to make room for approaches based on support and advocacy; to emphasise the key place of civil and human rights; to engage more readily with the views and experiences of more excluded and demonised groups of service users; to resist technical, managerial approaches to practice; and to build and sustain relationships with service users that are based on equality and respect rather than coercion and control.

Moving forward with users and carers

This chapter now turns to a discussion of the ways in which social workers can and do work alongside service users in ways that are 'liberatory' rather than 'regulatory' (Beresford and Croft, 2004, p 53). As we have shown earlier, government rhetoric is clear about the importance of user involvement but this message is clouded by ambiguity and contradiction. Individualisation and responsibilisation, regulation and control sit uncomfortably alongside partnership and participation, while social work remains hidebound by managerialism and the power of the market. We have already considered in this book the extent of the damage inflicted on social work, social workers and service users in the UK since the late 1970s. This is summarised effectively by Beresford and Croft (2004, p 63) as follows:

> The routine experience of social work and social services for many service users may be the same or even worse than 20 or 30 years ago. Assessment procedures have become even more mechanical and bureaucratic. 'Eligibility criteria' have become increasingly exclusionary. Disabled people can expect an ever-changing column of inadequately trained, appallingly paid care assistants. Child-care tragedies (reveal) the same problems of poor communication, management, resourcing and practice....There is a continuing lack of adequate, appropriate and reliable support for many.

Equally, though, we have emphasised the extent to which social work's heart remains; in its value base and in its stated commitment to emancipatory practice. Indeed, Chapters Four and Five gave us some insight into the ways in which social workers struggle in these uncertain and demanding times to keep the needs and rights of service users and carers at the centre of their practice. As Beresford and Croft (2004, p 56) argue, social work may be under extreme pressure – due to its loss of identity, the devaluing of practice, the dominance of managerialism and increasing globalisation and exclusion – but there are 'counter-developments' and user and carer involvement is an essential one.

Going the 'extra mile': working with and for service users and carers

This chapter now draws on the voices of service users and carers. We use a focus group discussion that we organised with service users and carers while we were preparing this book, as well as minutes of meetings from Stirling University User and Carer Involvement Group. Also, we refer to the work of academic colleagues and make links to material produced by other user groups and the national users' network. Our focus group involved: Mathew and Alan, mental health survivors; Monica and Jason, from a self-advocacy group for adults with learning disabilities; and Fiona and Colin, both carers (again all names have been changed to protect anonymity).

It may seem astounding to current students or newly qualified workers but the norm until relatively recently was for service users and carers to be excluded from key social work processes. For example, Julie, a lone parent who has received social work services on several occasions, had the following to say about her experience of a child protection conference:

> They said it was to discuss things but it was full of strangers and I didn't feel good in it. They used words I didn't understand and talked about me, not to me. Then afterwards … a social worker came out to see me and my son to check my house again … I broke down and told him everything but he seemed to think that things were OK and he signed me off their books and that was that. (Julie, as quoted in Cree and Davis, 2007, p 19)

Adult services are experienced similarly by some service users. Monica, who took part in the focus group for this book, had vivid memories of being 'sent' to a distant residential unit for adults with disabilities with no prior consultation. Although this took place more than 20 years ago, the feelings of outrage were still with her:

> 'I didn't have any say in where I was to go. They [social workers] did it all for me.... They think they know it all but they don't.'

Another focus group member, Colin, also described his experience of having social workers who did not share even basic information with him, despite his being a full-time carer:

'[The assessment] was a liaison between the CPN [community psychiatric nurse] and the social worker and there was a kind of breakdown in communication … I didn't know it was going to be happening and suddenly a social worker turned up on the doorstep to do a carers' assessment … out of the blue.'

Mathew had a recent experience of a social worker who spoke only to his partner, his carer:

'I don't think she said two words to me in my house, always spoke to my wife … she made you feel second class, she had no time for me … I was just there.'

Beresford and Croft (2004) suggest that social work has struggled over the years to balance both its liberatory and its reactionary potentials. The kind of practice described above by Julie, Monica, Colin and Mathew is, therefore, not something that just used to be. It happens now! Service users are, therefore, entitled to express negative views of social work and social workers. We know that, even when intentions are good, the reality for some service users is that social work gets it wrong. Meaningful participation requires that we hear and value what service users tell us, even when we do not like what they say. To do otherwise is to accord their voices an inferior status to those of professionals. As Forbes and Sashidharan (1997, p 496) suggest, 'the strength of a user position … is its opposition to present services and their underlying ideologies'. There is, then, little to be gained by silencing any 'oppositional voice' that users may have.

Box 6.4: 'It's not asking much, is it?' What service users want from social workers

Service users and carers have been telling us for several years now what they most appreciate in social workers and what they find extremely unhelpful (Skinner, 2001; Institute for Applied Health and Social Policy, 2002; Woodward, 2006, 2007; Beresford, 2007; Beresford et al, 2007; Cree and Davis, 2007; Doel and Best, 2008).

We could readily catalogue the negative side to social work as perceived by service users and carers but, instead, we choose to highlight the positive points that users and carers make.

Users and carers appreciate social workers who have the following skills:

- the ability to listen;
- the ability to communicate;
- the ability to advocate;
- the ability to work with other professionals;
- the ability to build strong relationships;
- the ability to share information.

Users and carers also value social workers who have the following qualities:

- reliability;
- consistency;
- staying power;
- patience;
- warmth;
- honesty;
- trustworthiness.

In addition, users and carers appreciate social workers who are:

- supportive;
- empathic;
- encouraging;
- attentive;
- caring;
- non-judgemental;
- knowledgeable about resources;
- upfront about professional power and responsibilities.

It is not surprising that service users and carers wish their social workers to be approachable, kind, respectful and well informed, and it seems that many practitioners are. Users and carers are provided with the information they need, they are listened to, their perspectives are valued and they are responded to in constructive ways. For some focus group members, whether their social workers listened and responded to them appropriately or not was down to the presence or absence of 'a calling'. Social workers and health professionals either demonstrated professional passion and personal commitment or they were just doing a job for the pay packet at the end of the month. Alan summed this up:

> '[I]n all professions … you get people who can talk to people and you get people that can't … you get people that are good at their job and you'll get people that are bad at their job … you can spot the ones that's in it for the money … and the ones that are in it because they want to be.'

The scenario, however, is rarely as straightforward as 'good' social worker or 'bad' social worker. Many users and carers also appreciate that professionals work under pressure due to constraints of time, money and bureaucracy. Beresford (2007), for example, highlights service users' understanding of the demands and challenges facing social workers. Focus group members too were familiar with some of the problems. For Mathew it was about overwork:

> '[T]hey've got a tight schedule, they've got probably seven or eight people to see that day.'

Colin saw the problem as bureaucratic:

> 'I think there's so many rules and regulations that they have to work by that they're just working to a rule book.'

Whatever the current policy and practice restrictions are – and we know there are many – the key point that service users are communicating is that workers have to believe in the importance of their role and task and in their ability to make a difference. We know that many workers can and do have a genuinely positive impact on the lives of service users (Cree and Davis, 2007; Doel and Best, 2008). In Mathew's words:

> 'I was part of an organisation … and she [social worker] was just absolutely brilliant, she'd all the time in the world for you … this person could talk to people and understood your illness.'

As Leone, who was a looked-after child and is now a social worker, says, despite the many difficulties she faced as a child and the inconsistencies in the support she received, good workers did make a difference to her life:

> I have to bring it back to the children's homes and the two workers who believed that I could do something, that I could be somebody. They went the extra mile with me, beyond the service offered as standard. (Leone, as quoted in Doel and Best, 2008, p 55)

An important message is being communicated by users and carers; good social work often depends on the qualities and skills of individual workers. This message is particularly significant for us, as we argue throughout this book that social workers at times cannot do the job for which they are educated because political, economic and organisational constraints will not allow them to do so. It seems, though, that some workers are more able, and more willing, than others to prioritise good practice, challenge oppression and discrimination and involve service users (Beresford and Croft, 2004). While there is room in the profession for many different kinds of social worker, we recognise the essential place of both core and emancipatory values (Higham, 2006) and of critical, where possible radical, ways of thinking and practising.

Service users and carers leading the way

Broadly speaking, users and carers are involved, especially within the voluntary sector, as trustees and volunteers. They sit on management committees and steering groups and are consulted when it comes to shaping strategy and evaluating services (NCVO, 2007). As a member of the organising committee of her local disabled people's social club, Louise, from the beginning of the chapter, is able to influence the programme of activities and to contribute to decisions about funding and support staff. This, unfortunately, only happens when she is supported to attend committee meetings and staff are not always available to do this. As discussed above, what involvement means for service users seems to depend on funding, management responsibilities and attitudes and the particular participation model being adopted (consumerist or democratic, for example). Also, while the organisational culture needs to be right for meaningful participation to take place (management need to support it and power relations need to be recognised and challenged), wider barriers to participation associated with personal, institutional, economic, cultural and political factors still need to be broken down (SCIE, 2007).

Beresford et al (2007) discuss the different ways in which they involved patients or service users in a study about their experiences of palliative care. Steering groups were used constructively to ensure that service users did not just take part in the research by answering questions but shaped the research process itself. As a result, research took place that appeared both ethical and sensitive to the needs and rights of people who were dying. This work by Beresford and his colleagues suggests ways in which service users and patients can become the 'co-producers of their own welfare' (Beresford et al, 2007, p 34); they both shaped the research and influenced the palliative services that they received. People who are dying and their carers may not represent most of those who come into contact with social work services. Equally, they are unlikely to be receiving services compulsorily. The significance of the research, however, is that it provides messages for all those who are looking to promote user and carer involvement and participation in significant ways.

A similarly positive message is communicated by Puigvert and Elboj (2004), who provide an account of the way in which particularly powerless and excluded women were supported to regain control of their lives and the services they received. The lives and experiences of the Spanish women discussed here relate directly to those of many of the women who come into contact with social work services in the UK: 'With little or no formal education and limited social opportunities, they face a dual form of exclusion in silence: as women and for not having educational qualifications' (Puigvert and Elboj, 2004, p 351).

Granted the work being done to support excluded women to find their voices took place mainly in adult education centres, away from the more socially and personally controlling culture of social services departments. Again, however, the implications for social work practice that seeks to work alongside marginalised users and carers in productive ways are clear. We can try to build 'spaces that promote people's capacities and recognise their realities versus focusing on deficits [and this] can make the difference between facilitating personal and social transformation, versus perpetuating or creating a low self-image and passivity' (Puigvert and Elboj, 2004, p 355).

Refugees and asylum seekers

In the UK it is hard to find a group more marginalised than refugees and asylum seekers. As Kohli (2007) argues, any discussion about refugees and asylum seekers is obscured by 'the noise and heat of political opinions and policy debates concerning asylum seekers and refugees' (Kohli, 2007, p x). For Cemlyn and Briskman (2003), however, any debate that does take place is heavily influenced by the extent to which policy is underpinned by racist and punitive notions. In this unforgiving climate, official social work responses to refugees and asylum seekers are, at best, inconsistent and, at worst, downright harmful (Humphries, 2004a, 2004b). For example, a report published in 2007 by the Refugee Council provided a voice for asylum-seeking women in Scotland (RWSG, 2007). Waiting to hear about their application for asylum was a particularly anxiety-provoking experience for these women but this was compounded by social isolation due to their separation from family and culture and their stigmatised status; little opportunity to work or receive education and training; experiences of direct and institutional racism; and a lack of information about their rights and the services available to them, including childcare and legal representation.

Social work is only one of the many services that refugees and asylum seekers could have contact with. Given social work's stated commitment to social justice it might be reasonably expected that the profession would lead the way in empowering practice with refugees and asylum seekers. If we take the case of asylum-seeking children, however, it is apparent that, despite legal responsibilities to assess all children in need (1989 Children Act; 1995 Children Scotland Act), many asylum-seeking children are receiving incomplete or even non-existent social work support (Stanley, 2001; Refugee Council, 2002; Cemlyn and Briskman, 2003; Humphries, 2004a). Social workers are put in a difficult situation, certainly, with their duty to report to immigration services anyone they consider to be 'bogus' (2002 National Immigration and Asylum Act) and the expectation that social services will only work with asylum seekers if 'absolutely necessary' (Collett, 2004). However, social work's traditional emphasis on 'personal weaknesses' and its 'individualised understanding of problems ... at the expense of structural explanations' continue to sideline issues of power and privilege generally and to marginalise black people's experiences of racism particularly (Graham, 2007, p 22). As long as social work is prepared to support dominant deficit and assimilation models for understanding and responding to the needs of black people generally (Penketh, 2000; Bernard, 2002; Graham 2007), it will be difficult for the profession to challenge the political and media portrayal of refugees and asylum seekers as 'criminals, terrorists and scroungers' (Collett, 2004, p 79).

Hayes and Humphries (2004a, p 219) conclude that 'It has ... become clear that social workers are now very much part of the army of workers in both the national and local state who, without their consent, indirectly and directly, form part of the internal policing of immigration'.

There are, though, good examples of social work with refugees and asylum seekers across the UK (Brown, C., 2004; Wells and Hoikkala, 2004; Kohli, 2007). Helpful services, both voluntary and statutory, are based on advocacy, support and advice and are underpinned by a commitment to listening to and valuing the experiences of refugees and asylum seekers and to combating racist and stigmatising policy and practice. There are also examples of refugees and asylum seekers coming together with paid workers and volunteers to raise awareness of the injustices often faced by people who are new to the UK. Although social workers tend not to be heavily involved in such organisations, there is much that can be learned from their approach. Take Positive Action in Housing (www.paih.org), a housing agency for minority ethnic people in Scotland, as an example. The agency is minority ethnic-led and campaigns for everyone to have equal rights to housing and to a life free from discrimination and racial harassment. Speaking out about the dispersal, detention and deportation of refugees and asylum seekers, the agency has succeeded in bringing many individuals and communities into the struggle for equal rights and recognition (Qureshi, 2007). There may well be more opportunity for non-governmental organisations (NGOs) like Positive Action in Housing to influence policy (Spencer, 2006) – they are less likely than their local government counterparts to be mired in care–control dilemmas. Equally, however, as was explored in Chapter Five, the NGO sector does not hold the monopoly on good practice.

Advocacy

Henderson and Pochin (2001) discuss the wide range of advocacy schemes to be found in the UK. These schemes tend to be run loosely on one or more of the following models: professionally funded and run (professional casework advocacy); generically focused and supported by volunteers (volunteer advocacy); based on citizen advocacy models (citizen advocacy, in which a volunteer advocate is partnered on a long-term basis with a particular citizen or partner); user-led (self-advocacy); or informally based on relationships between two or more peers (peer advocacy, where people sharing similar problems or concerns come together to advocate for themselves). While it is apparent that there is plenty of advocacy taking place in the UK, it seems that few agree about what advocacy is, how it is best achieved or how much use it is (Henderson and Pochin, 2001). This said, in 2002, the then London-based, but now England and Wales-wide, agency, Action for Advocacy (www.actionforadvocacy.org.uk), published an advocacy charter following consultation with many advocacy organisations. The charter now defines advocacy as 'taking action to help people say what they want, secure their rights, represent their interests and obtain services they need. Advocates and advocacy schemes work in partnership with the people they support and take their side' (Action for Advocacy, 2002, p 2).

    That marginalised or vulnerable people require an individual or group to advocate independently on their behalf is supported by government in the UK (for example, Scottish Executive, 2001b; DH, 2002b). Advocacy is seen as a way in which oppressed people can secure choice, justice, support, protection, social development, access to services and a general sense of empowerment (Henderson and Pochin, 2001, p 145). In this way, while not traditional social work, advocacy shares many of its principles and values with social work (Forbat and Atkinson, 2005). Also, advocacy has been recognised recently as one of several core social work roles (Higham, 2006). Successful advocacy, however, is that which truly aligns itself with the needs and rights of oppressed and marginalised people. Returning to the long-recognised conflict in social work that results directly from its 'dual mandate' (Powell, 2001) to both care and control, tensions inevitably arise when social work tries to accommodate an advocacy role alongside its duties to assess need and risk and to protect vulnerable people and wider communities (Forbat and Atkinson, 2005). Dalrymple (2003, p 1047) also notes that, 'while advocacy is a focus of the modernizing agenda, it is increasingly difficult for health and social welfare practitioners to take on this role', due to the increasing emphasis on bureaucracy and risk management. Advocacy, therefore, becomes the remit of independent sector agencies. Independent advocacy is, as Dalrymple (2003) argues, an important service, which promotes the voice and agency of, in this case, young people. Equally, though, there seems to be some danger in advocacy becoming something that professionals do to, rather than with, service users (Forbat and Atkinson, 2005).

User-led, self-advocacy agencies, like People First (people with learning disabilities advocating on their own behalf), seem more likely than professionally led services to enable groups of users to find a collective voice (Hoy et al, 2006) and to build personal confidence and self-worth (Docherty et al, 2006). As Monica, a focus group member says:

> 'I'm a user and like everybody else I need a bit of help here and there but we've got voices and [I'm] a person now … I challenge!'

There is, though, some concern about the extent to which self-advocates are only able to speak up about the services society is willing to offer them, rather than those they really need or desire (Aspis, 1997). In this respect, advocacy, like other developments in, or facets of, the user participation agenda, requires critical appraisal. Our own focus group, though, stressed the extent to which user and carer movements, and the collective advocacy that goes hand in hand with them, are helping both groups and individuals to move forward. As Alan says, "there's safety in numbers", a view that was echoed by all and summed up neatly by Mathew:

> '[A] few voices are stronger than one voice and I think the authorities listen to us now. Up to 10 year ago, they told you what to eat, when to sleep [but] you've an opinion now and places like [Organisation X – a community of people whose lives are affected by longer-term mental ill-health] has made a great difference to me.'

As Dalrymple (2003, 2004) suggests, advocacy for and with children is a particularly complex subject, because the children's participation agenda generally is characterised by contradiction. We already noted in Chapter Three the extent to which UK society has yet to decide whether children are in need of protection or control. Similarly, in Chapter Four we highlighted the extent to which individualising and responsibilising approaches tend to characterise social work with young people who are troubled and troublesome. There is, however, some evidence that children can benefit from advocacy specifically, and participation developments more generally (Franklin and Sloper, 2004; Pithouse and Crowley, 2007). The challenge, though, is in 'Shifting the balance of complaints and advocacy from a narrow adult-oriented focus around welfare issues to a more child-centred and child-led process that promotes authentic voice and rights' (Pithouse and Crowley, 2007, p 211).

Service user involvement: breaking down the barriers

Box 6.5: What service user movement?

The comments below belong to Miranda Moreland, who posted them on the BBC's Action Network website in 2007:

It would seem to be a complete fallacy stating that there is a Service User Movement in this country.... The Government, NHS and Mental Health Charities are surely over the moon that it does not exist ... we can't possibly have the Lunatics taking over the Asylum now can we!!!

The struggle we find ourselves in is ridiculous. Up against bureaucracy the whole time. To be paid our travelling expenses is like trying to extract blood from a stone. We are hardly welcomed when we do attend. We have to write separate letters to ask if we may please have a free place at a conference ... we wouldn't be asking for a free place if we could afford to come! And it is humiliating to feel we are begging which puts so many Service Users off that they don't participate at all.... Our ideas are not minuted but within about 6 months our ideas are suddenly part of the new structure and probably bringing in some form of new funding as pamphlets are being written and papers produced on the very subject matter that we were ignored over when we first brought it to the table. (Moreland, 2007)

Ms Moreland sounds to have had enough of trying to influence mental health policy and practice and, certainly, if things are as bad as she sees them, there is still a very long way to go. Branfield et al (2006) studied the extent to which the user involvement agenda is actually having an impact on service users, in terms of their ability to network, to build sources of support and to work together to achieve change. The authors emphasise the extent to which individual service users feel that they benefit from being part of a users' organisation: company and communication with others; insight into their own difficulties; opportunities to help others; strength in numbers; and having something with a purpose to occupy them. User organisations were, however, rarely genuinely user led. In disability groups, for example, the workers and managers were usually non-disabled. Users also found it difficult to keep groups going. There were a few key activists who participated regularly but attendance at meetings was generally poor and recruitment was difficult. It is important, however, to avoid assumptions about homogeneity among service users as much as it is to avoid suppositions about there being only one kind of social worker. Users themselves recognise that not all disabled people are the same and that, even if some experiences are shared, not everyone wants to hang out together (Branfield et al, 2006).

From Branfield et al's (2006) study it is apparent that one of the barriers to meaningful participation that users found most difficult to break down was that associated with poor and inconsistent funding, which sets groups against each other as they compete for money from central and local government. In addition, small groups, especially those that were user led and had a minority ethnic focus, felt that they could never compete with the five-star voluntary sector agencies that sucked up the bulk of public funds. There was also an enormous hurdle for users to climb when it came to persuading professionals that their knowledge, their evidence, was at least equally as valid as the professional perspective. Branfield et al (2006) emphasise just how difficult it is still for service users to get their point across, despite all the attention paid in policy, practice and academic circles, to 'hearing users' voices. The barriers were summarised by service users thus (Branfield et al, 2006, p 31): the devaluing of service user knowledge; problems of access and tokenism; the culture of health and social care organisations; and resource issues. In the words of Ms Moreland (2007) again, 'Unless we are truly integrated into the professionals very existence as part of normal life we will always have a situation of them and us, causing the all too familiar faces of stigma and discrimination from the very people who should know better'.

Conclusion: taking user involvement forward in social work

Much of the academic literature on service user and carer involvement is based on voluntary sector projects and services. Certainly, Beresford et al's (2007) account of specialist palliative care social work demonstrates that branches of social work can provide services that meet service users' needs. The users and patients who took part in this study emphasised the importance of partnership working, accessible and flexible services, and workers who know how to build effective relationships based on friendliness, honesty, reciprocity, caring and understanding. Beresford et al (2007) demonstrate equally the extent to which mainstream social work, especially in the state sector, has been, and is being, taken down a different road altogether as bureaucratic and managerial processes take a firm hold. In 1997, Forbes and Sashidharan argued that social work would struggle to take the user involvement agenda forward as long as:

> one strand of social work rhetoric speaks of the need for user empowerment, self advocacy and anti-oppressive practice [while], at the same time, social work has become increasingly driven by the exigencies of economic cuts, scarcity of resources, legislative and administrative reform, leading to a more procedural practice aimed at tighter social regulation. (1997, p 490)

Echoing this, we have emphasised throughout this book the extent to which social workers find themselves in places they would rather not be; in situations that leave them with little in the way of job satisfaction and which push them to compromise their professional values and personal convictions. The workers who took part in the focus groups for this book were trying their best to 'go the extra mile'. They did so, however, while feeling resentful, and at times anxious and exhausted, by the numerous demands of the job, which they were adamant were associated with externally imposed constraints and not with service users' needs. In the current climate, the only aspects of potentially radical practice that workers could see were a willingness to build productive working relationships with service users, to identify with their wider oppression and to keep asking questions of management. Very little was mentioned about hearing, valuing and acting on the views of service users and one suspects that there is, in reality, little time or energy to promote authentic user involvement in social work.

In this chapter, we have shown that service users and carers have already told us much about what they look for in social workers, in terms of the professional and personal qualities required. Also, we have provided some examples of initiatives that seem to place users and carers centre-stage although specific social work examples were more difficult to find. The voices of service users and carers included here reflect the extent to which services are inconsistent in their adoption of inclusive and empowering approaches. Equally, users and carers are clear that committed individuals in social work and social care can and do make a difference to their lives.

Chapters Four and Five emphasised that tenacious, politically astute, critical thinkers do remain in social work but the conclusion to this chapter has to address the extent to which user and carer involvement remains problematic for the social work profession. In a service provision culture changed beyond recognition by marketisation and managerialism, there is a risk that service user and carer involvement becomes one challenge too many for hard-pressed workers. If we agree, however, that social work is about social justice and making a difference to people's lives then genuine user and carer involvement is a vital part of the professional role and task. The core of our argument is that working alongside service users in meaningful ways, identifying with their struggles and aspirations and acting purposefully on what they say, is not impossible in social work settings, even those that are immersed in social control responsibilities and in the political and media spotlight as a result.

Questions for discussion

➲   The involvement of service users and carers in the design and evaluation of social work services has become a key theme in British social policy. What do you see as the main reasons for the emergence of this theme?

➲   In terms of your own practice experiences, are service users generally viewed as 'friends', 'foes' or a political 'fetish' (Cowden and Singh, 2007; see suggestions for further reading below)?

➲   Social workers and service users are often viewed in terms of a 'them and us' dichotomy. Is the gulf between social workers, service users and carers as real as some might imagine?

Suggestions for further reading

➲   Beresford, P., Adshead, L. and Croft, S. (2007) *Palliative Care, Social Work and Service Users: Making Life Possible*, London: Jessica Kingsley Publishers. A unique book in two ways: because it focuses on the under-researched area of palliative care and because it explores the topic from service users' perspectives. This book is uplifting, not only because it is based on genuine user and carer involvement in research and practice but also because it illustrates good social work practice in action.

➲   Doel, M. and Best, L. (2008) *Experiencing Social Work, Learning from Service Users*, London: Sage Publications. Using the voices of people who use social work services, this book demonstrates what we can learn from service users and carers and how good social work has to be linked to a wider quest for social justice.

➲   Graham, M. (2007) *Black Issues in Social Work and Social Care*, Bristol: The Policy Press. Placing black people's perspectives at the centre, this book argues that, so far, anti-discriminatory frameworks for practice have not taken sufficient account of black people's values, experiences and views of the world. The author, however, by offering a rethink of social divisions and oppression, suggests creative and achievable ways forward.

➲   Taylor, J., Williams, V., Johnson, R., Hiscutt, I. and Brennan, M. (2007) *We Are Not Stupid*, London: People First Lambeth/ Shaping Our Lives, www.shapingourlives.org.uk/documents/ wansweb.pdf. Five adults who have a learning disability provide powerful accounts of their everyday experiences, offering their views on a range of issues including relationships, independence and support staff. They conclude that all they want is an ordinary life but that, to date, not enough has been done by government to break down practical and attitudinal barriers.

Rediscovering collective approaches

7

Box 7.1: Sandra

Sandra is employed as a community worker in a Community Health Partnership in a large northern town. Part of her work involves supporting carers of people with learning disabilities. When the local council announces that it intends to close down several local day centres as part of its modernisation strategy of developing more 'personalised' services, carers' groups are incensed. Alongside service user groups and trade unions, they organise a campaign to prevent the closures, arguing that the centres play an important social role and that the council's main concern in closing them is with saving money. In response, the council brands this campaign 'reactionary' and based on an outmoded view of learning disability. Sandra's feeling is that while some carers may have paternalistic attitudes, the majority want to see more progressive services. They are, however, genuinely concerned that if the centres are closed, their sons and daughters will soon become isolated. She wants to support this campaign but is aware that she could be placing herself in a dangerous position if she appears to be working against her own employer.

Introduction

For many social workers in Britain today, the dilemmas facing Sandra may not arise for the simple reason that most, if not all, of their work will be with individuals rather than groups (and perhaps not even that, since, as we saw in Chapter Four, one of the main complaints of social workers today is the limited opportunities even for direct work with individuals). Where individuals do work with groups, in areas such as criminal justice, for example, the focus is likely to be on changing the behaviour of individuals, perhaps using cognitive-behavioural approaches, rather than addressing unmet need or challenging inappropriate services. Yet historically, collective approaches have been at the heart of progressive social work approaches, in three distinct ways.

First, as we saw in Chapter Two, community development approaches have been part of social work since its inception in the late 19th century, in the form of the Settlement movement. Both Mullaly (1997) and Powell (2001) locate the origins of the progressive, radical strand of social work in the humanitarian, collectivist approach that the Settlement movement espoused. While, as we also saw in that chapter, there were definite limits to that humanitarianism, the Settlement movement did nevertheless offer an alternative of sorts to the individualised, victim-blaming approach practised by the Charity Organisation Society (COS). That collective tradition was rediscovered in the late 1960s, but this time in a considerably radicalised form as a result of the influence of both the social movements of the period and the libertarian ideas and strategies of writers like the American activist, Saul Alinsky. The first section of this chapter will explore the relevance of such collective approaches to social work today.

The second way in which collective approaches have been important for social work is through the influence of social movements on social work practice and services. The origins of anti-oppressive practice, for example, lie in the powerful social movements of women, black people and gay people that developed in the late 1960s and early 1970s (fuelled also by the trade union struggles of these years). More recently, the disability movement and the mental health service users' movement have been responsible for providing the social models of health and disability that are now core features of social work theory and practice. In addition, the impetus for more user-led forms of service delivery, including Independent Living Centres and mental health crisis centres, has often come from service user groups, sometimes working in partnership with like-minded professionals. In the next section, we shall explore what relevance contemporary social movements might have for the development of a radical practice.

Finally, as many workers have found through experience, and as Sandra's dilemma outlined earlier indicates, it can be difficult, and, from an employment point of view, potentially hazardous, to practise radical social work in isolation. Collective organisation within the workplace is essential not just as a means of protecting wages and conditions but also as a way of offering protection against the attempts of some managers to curb forms of practice that they see as challenging their policies or priorities. In some cases, such practice will be concerned with securing additional financial resources for groups of service users; in others, the challenge will be to eradicate policies that are clearly incompatible with core social work values. As we write, for example, a national campaign is under way for the reinstatement of community psychiatric nurse and union activist Karen Riesman, sacked by her employers for speaking out against the privatisation of mental health services in Manchester where she worked. More generally, in the context of increasing managerial control and the deprofessionalisation of social work we discussed in Chapter Three, simply adhering to core values and notions of ethical practice can carry risks. Traditionally, such collective organisation has taken two forms: professional and trade union. The potential and limitations of both to contemporary social work will be considered in the final section.

Challenging 'case-ism'

Writing in 1943, the radical American sociologist C. Wright Mills noted:

> Present institutions train several kinds of person – such as judges and social workers – to think in terms of 'situations'. Their activities and mental outlook are set within the existing norms of society: in their professional work they tend to have occupationally trained incapacity to rise above 'cases'. (Mills, 1943, p 171)

Such 'case-ism' – the tendency to see people using services in isolation from the communities in which they live and from the structural factors that shape their lives – was the object of the radical critique of case work in the 1970s. Radical social work, by contrast, meant precisely 'Understanding the position of the oppressed in the context of the social and economic structure they live in' (Bailey and Brake, 1975, p 9).

As Bailey and Brake emphasised (and as others have argued since; Fook, 1993) such an approach did not have to involve a rejection of case work per se. Rather, their critique was focused on those forms of case work that involved 'blaming the victim' by consistently locating the source of individuals' problems in their alleged moral or developmental deficits while ignoring the poverty and oppression that formed the backdrop to their lives. That said, in practice the 1970s saw many social workers who wished to engage in more progressive forms of work looking towards approaches, including community development and community social work approaches, that incorporated structural analyses and collective responses. Such approaches have become much less common in state social work practice in recent times, mainly due to the dominance of care management approaches since the early 1990s. Arguably a new form of 'case-ism' has replaced the psychosocial 'case-ism' of the 1950s and 1960s. As we have seen, however, profound dissatisfaction with care management approaches, as expressed both in official reports (Scottish Executive, 2006a) and in research into the views and experiences of frontline workers (Jones, 2001; Dustin, 2007), has fuelled a desire for a return to more holistic, value-based forms of practice. The fact also that problems of poverty, inequality and stigma affect the lives of service users no less today than they did three decades ago suggests that the time is ripe for revisiting the role of collective approaches in social work.

Community work: dilemmas and possibilities

To return to the case example, Sandra's role as a community worker is to work with groups of service users and carers to help them collectively identify their needs and work with them to achieve these needs – a community development approach. According to one definition:

> Community development is directed at people who feel excluded from society. It consists of a set of methods which can broaden vision and capacity for social change, and approaches, including consultation, advocacy and relationships with local groups. It is a way of working, informed by certain principles which seek to encourage communities – people who live in the same areas or who have something else in common – to tackle themselves the problems which they face and identify to be important which aim to empower them to change things by developing their own skills, knowledge and experience and also working in partnership with other groups and statutory agencies. The way in which such changes are achieved is crucial and so both the task and the process is important. (DHSS, cited in Sharkey, 2000, p 7)

In different times and places, community development approaches have been both very conservative (Mayo, 1975) and very radical (Ledwith, 2005). Yet the fact that they are concerned with *collective* responses to *collective* problems often means that it is easier to make the links to wider political and structural issues than is the case with individual approaches.

Four features of the scenario outlined above commonly face workers and groups adopting a community development approach. First, there is the issue of *problem definition*. In this example, based on a real dispute that took place in the West of Scotland in 2007, the council is seeking to define the problem as being the continued existence of old-fashioned, paternalistic services based on a medical view of learning disability, which deny individuals with learning disabilities the right to independent living. The carers' groups and trade unions, by contrast, know that the council is desperately short of money and believe that it is seeking to make savings by outsourcing services and making staff redundant. The issue, therefore, concerns the nature of the 'personalisation' approaches currently being promoted by governments both north and south of the border. Are such approaches best seen as a way of extending service user choice or, conversely, are they a means of transferring risk and responsibility from the local authority to individual service users (Ferguson, 2007)?

Such disputes over problem definition are common within community work approaches. In one well-documented case study from the 1970s, hundreds of tenants living in newly built council houses in the Gorbals area of Glasgow experienced common problems of dampness, with water streaming down their walls, wallpaper peeling off, fungus spores developing on their carpets and, in some cases, an infestation of spider-like insects (Bryant and Bryant, 1982). The council's response to their complaints was to argue that the problem was not dampness (which implied some structural defect in the design of the buildings) but rather 'condensation', due to the tenants' failure to use their new heating systems properly. In the end, following a vigorous campaign that lasted over several years and that was supported by a local community work student unit, the tenants were successful in persuading the council that the problem was indeed a structural one (they proved that the housing was based on a Tunisian housing model, with insufficient attention paid to the rather obvious differences between the climates of North Africa and the West of Scotland). As a result, the flats were demolished and the tenants rehoused in alternative, dry housing.

The experience of the Gorbals Anti-Dampness Campaign, as it was known, like that of Sandra and the carers' groups with whom she is working, highlights a second feature of the use of collective approaches in social work. They often directly confront issues of *power*. This does not mean that winning the moral and intellectual argument is not also important. In the Gorbals case, for example, a huge body of evidence – legal, public health, building construction – was assembled to support the tenants' case, often drawing on the expertise of sympathetic professionals in these disciplines. Similarly, in the example earlier, the carers' groups and the trade unions would need to demonstrate that the council's plans would indeed have the damaging effects that they are alleging, not least if they are to win over public opinion. In neither case, however, is it likely that good arguments by themselves would be sufficient to change council policy, unless they are backed up by other forms of pressure. In this sense, too, community work approaches are often seen as more 'political' than individual or group work approaches.

Third, collective approaches often raise issues of *professional accountability*. During the 1970s and into the early 1980s, many community workers would have shared the views of radical writers like the American community work activist Saul Alinsky (1971) in seeing their primary allegiance as being to the groups with whom they were working, rather than to their employer (in theory, if not always in practice!). The very real risk of losing your job by challenging your employer's policies in the much harsher political climate of the 1980s and 1990s, however, understandably made many workers more cautious about doing so. Community workers in the West of Scotland, for example, were expressly prohibited from becoming involved in the huge community-based campaign against Margaret Thatcher's Poll Tax in the late 1980s. Similarly, Sandra would need to walk a tightrope between giving support to the carers' groups with whom she is working and not appearing to be overtly challenging her employer's policies.

Fourth, the case example highlights what is sometimes referred to as the 'dual objectives' of community work approaches (Twelvetrees, 1982). The carers with whom Sandra is working are concerned that the closure of the day centres and their replacement by more individualised, 'personalised' services will reduce the quality of life of their relatives, particularly their opportunities for social interaction. Their main goal, therefore, is to prevent these closures, although a more immediate goal is to persuade the council to enter into negotiations to address their concerns. In community work terminology, these would be referred to as *product* goals. In addition, however, as the experience of countless community-based and workplace-based campaigns show, in the process of engaging in such action, people often change: they learn new skills such as speaking at meetings, they develop a greater awareness of the role of local politicians and the media, and they gain a greater confidence in themselves and their abilities. These are sometimes referred to as the *process* goals of community work. Part of Sandra's role as a worker would be to support this process by maximising the opportunities for involvement and helping group members to reflect on all aspects of the campaign, including the need to avoid paternalism and ensure that the views and wishes of service users are fully recognised. Within the radical model of community work developed by the Brazilian Paulo Freire (Freire, 1996), this process is known as *conscientisation*, or 'education for critical consciousness', defined by Whitmore and Wilson (2004, p 201) as:

> the development, through dialogue, of awareness of one's reality and engaging in critical thinking about it as process, as transformation, rather than as something static and unchangeable.... Implicit in all this is the assumption that every human being is capable of understanding complex phenomena, engaging in an interactive process with others to develop a critical analysis of their reality, and individually and collectively taking action to change their world.

In these four respects, the issues facing Sandra will be very similar to those that faced workers employing a community development approach in the 1970s. In other ways, however, her work is likely to be different from theirs. Then, the focus of community work in the UK was often on the geographical community and frequently involved work around housing issues. Now, it is more likely to involve users of community care services, such as older people, people with mental health problems or carers' groups.

In part, this is because much council housing was sold off during the 1980s as part of the Conservative Party's Right to Buy policy, making collective organisation around housing issues more difficult. In part, however, it is because the community care policies of the last few decades mean that many people who would previously have lived in institutions now live in the community, where they have often developed strong collective organisations. In the area of learning difficulties, for example, People First describes itself as 'an organisation run by and for people with learning difficulties to raise awareness of and campaign for the rights of people with learning difficulties and to support self-advocacy groups across the country' (www.peoplefirstltd. com). While such groups will often describe their ideas and activities in the language of 'collective advocacy', in many respects they closely resemble the community development approaches of earlier periods.

A second difference from the 1970s is that, according to one leading theorist, community work under New Labour presents a picture of 'conditional development' (Popple, 2006). Positively, Popple argues, over the past few years New Labour governments have increased funding for community development projects and strategies, for example through a Community Empowerment Fund and Local Strategic Partnerships, as part of their strategy for reducing social exclusion. Less positively, however, such funding is usually delivered within an overall framework of top-down, market-driven 'modernisation', with government priorities often very different from those of local people. The result can be that:

> Where communities are at odds with new Labour and contest their 'modernizing' policies, such as in the case of the closure of the Govanhill Pool in Glasgow (Mooney and Fyfe, 2004), they can be sidelined. This can place community development workers in difficult situations where they have to balance their responsibilities to their employers with the expressed needs of local communities. (Popple, 2006, p 7)

As we saw, this is exactly the dilemma that faced Sandra in the vignette at the start of this chapter!

Benefits and challenges

What benefits might service users gain from the use of community development approaches by social workers and what challenges might face workers who wish to practise in this way? Their most obvious strength lies in their potential to be *preventive*, as the following 'parable' suggests.

> **Box 7.2: A parable about problem solving**
>
> A person standing near a river hears a call for help and sees someone drowning. He jumps in and pulls the struggling swimmer out of the water and resuscitates him. As he finishes resuscitating the first swimmer, a second cries out. Again, he enters the water and with great effort hauls the second drowning person ashore. A third person calls out for help and he jumps to the rescue and nearly drowns in the effort, but manages to pull the third person out of the river. An admiring crowd has gathered when a fourth person calls for help and our hero walks away. 'Where are you going? What about this person who is drowning?' He turns and says, 'I'm tired of rescuing people from the river. I'm going upstream to find out who's pushing them in!' (McGourty and Chasnoff, 2003)

The message is clear: addressing structural problems at source will often reduce or remove the need for individualised, remedial work further down the line. As Preston-Shoot (2007, p 60) notes:

> Unemployment, poor housing, poverty, inadequate community resources and high eligibility criteria all impinge on clients of social work agencies. If social workers neglect these features, they omit an important, influential part of the reality of their clients' lives and limit the extent and impact of their change efforts.

In reality, of course, the limited sources of power available both to social workers and to local community groups mean that the 'targets of change' may be fairly localised and small-scale. Such changes, however, can still have a real impact on the lives of those involved. The experience of one of us, for example, of working for several years as a case worker with a large number of lone parents in a deprived area of Glasgow led to the conclusion that good after-school care services and babysitting services might do more to improve the mental health and quality of life of these parents than an individual case work approach could achieve. Subsequently, working with groups of lone parents over a period of time led to the establishment of a fully funded sitter service, which enabled many of these parents to undertake further education or simply have a night out, away from their children.

A second strength of such approaches – their *process* aspect – is their capacity for bringing about positive change in those involved. At the most basic level, collective approaches can help to reduce people's sense of isolation and powerlessness, whether as mental health service users, lone parents or older people. The realisation that other people have to deal with the same problems, and that these problems are often the product of stigma and discrimination rather than some inherent weakness or deficit, can be extremely empowering. As Sally French suggests:

> Perhaps the most important aspect of the disability movement is the powerful impact it has had on disabled people themselves. Disabled people have been internally oppressed by their conditioning. This has given rise to negative feelings about themselves and other disabled people. One of the major achievements of the disability movement is the support it offers disabled people in ridding themselves of this oppression. (cited in Campbell and Oliver, 1996, pp 177–8)

Challenges

Our experience both as social work educators and as organisers of critical social work conferences is that many students and workers would like to be able to employ such collective approaches. They feel, however, that both the current managerial ethos and the organisational structure of social work departments – in particular, the purchaser–provider split – make it impossible for them to do so. Certainly, there do appear to be more opportunities for employing such approaches, including collective advocacy, in the voluntary sector. Another area where community development principles and practice have survived and even grown is health promotion and community health. That said, even within statutory social work there is some evidence that the climate may be becoming more conducive. In particular, both north and south of the border, policy documents lay increasing stress on the importance of preventive approaches. Concepts of prevention and early intervention are central to the recommendations of *Changing Lives* (Scottish Executive, 2006a), the report of the 21st-Century Review of Social Work in Scotland. That report also argues that:

> Community social work has, in the past, been promoted as a discrete activity, conducted apart from mainstream social work practice. A new approach is now needed, which positions social work services at the heart of communities delivering a combination of individual and community based work alongside education, housing, health and police services. (Scottish Executive, 2006a, p 38)

What this suggests, as we have argued elsewhere in this book, is that the current widespread dissatisfaction with social work as currently practised is opening up spaces for more challenging forms of practice, including community development approaches.

Social movements and social work

A second aspect of collective approaches within social work concerns the relationship between social work and social movements. As we saw in Chapter Two, in the 1970s, contact with social movements such as the women's movement and the disability movement was important in deepening social work's commitment to anti-oppressive practice (see also Thompson, 2002). For reasons also discussed in that chapter, for much of the 1980s and 1990s, there was less opportunity for such contact. However, the rise of new social movements over the past decade is creating new opportunities and, in this section, we will consider how three contemporary examples of social movements might similarly inform social work practice in the 21st century.

The mental health users' movement

The 1980s and 1990s saw the emergence in Britain of the mental health service users' movement, similar to the larger disability movement that developed in the same period (Rogers and Pilgrim, 1991; Campbell, 1996). Unlike the professional-led anti-psychiatry movement that flourished in the 1960s, this new movement is made up primarily of people who have experienced mental distress and who have often had experience of the psychiatric system (Barnes and Shardlow, 1996). At the same time, the movement works closely with non-service users or 'allies' (often mental health professionals). As Beresford (2005) notes, for example, the campaign against government proposals to severely restrict the civil liberties of people with mental health problems in England and Wales in the first decade of the 21st century involved a very wide range of organisations in a loose coalition called the Mental Health Alliance. The coalition included:

> Church, community, civil rights, Black and minority ethnic, mental health, charitable, service users and professional organisations, including the Royal College of Psychiatrists. Proposals for extending compulsion have probably led to more campaigning activity, including pickets, demonstrations and marches, than any other previous issue. (Beresford, 2005, pp 13-14)

Alongside such campaigning activities, mental health service users' organisations have influenced social work and healthcare in three distinct if related areas.

Social work education

A requirement of the new social work qualification introduced in 2004 is that programme providers demonstrate evidence of service user involvement in all aspects of the programme including selection, teaching and assessment. Our experience at Stirling and at other Scottish universities is that local mental health service users have played a prominent part in this process, due in part to the strength of their organisations, with the result that they are currently involved in most aspects of teaching relating to mental health.

Services

The expansion of the voluntary sector in the early 1990s allowed for the development of community-based mental health services outside the psychiatric system in which service users often play an active role. These include advocacy services, crisis services based on a social model of crisis, new approaches to work with people with a diagnosis of schizophrenia (Hearing Voices groups) and work-related services, most notably the Clubhouse Model. It would be wrong to romanticise these models or to exaggerate their significance in a mental health system still dominated by professional psychiatry and biomedical approaches. In addition, as we saw in Chapter Five, these organisations are often funded on a shoestring and should not be seen as a substitute for a well-organised, properly funded mental health system. Nevertheless, based as they often are on the individual and collective experience of mental health service users, they do give a glimpse of alternative, more holistic, ways of responding to mental distress.

Mental health policy

Reference was made earlier to the part played by mental health service users in challenging mental health policy in England and Wales. In Scotland, the experience seems to have been a more productive one, with mental health service users' groups actively involved in the construction of the parallel legislation north of the border. The result is that the 2003 Scottish Act includes a range of provisions including advance statements and advocacy services that the users' movement has campaigned for over many years, as well as being based on a set of principles that enshrine empowering practice in this field. (By way of qualification, however, it should be noted that the Act also reflects the dominant 'public safety' discourse in introducing compulsory treatment in the community orders.)

Asylum seekers

As we saw in the previous chapter, few sections of society have experienced greater demonisation, abuse and denial of human rights in recent years than those seeking asylum from persecution and war. Despite the fact that their rights are enshrined in United Nations Conventions, asylum seekers and refugees have frequently experienced the most extreme forms of social exclusion, including harassment from governments, racist groups and local people whose fears are often fanned by right-wing tabloid newspapers. Given social work's avowed commitment to human rights and anti-oppressive practice, one might have expected that social workers would be in the forefront of defending this vulnerable group. In fact, the silence of the social work profession on this issue over the past decade has been deafening. In a scathing critique, Humphries (2004b, p 102), after describing the poverty and trauma experienced by so many asylum seekers, argues:

> On the face of it these are all conditions that require social work intervention, and one would expect social workers and other state officials to protest at the low level of subsistence – lower than that of their poorest clients – imposed on people who have already endured the traumas forcing them to leave their country of origin, and the stress of finding their way to and dealing with living in a new country. There is very little evidence of this having happened.

Against the stream, a small number of social work academics and practitioners in Britain, Australia, Greece, Slovenia and elsewhere *have* sought to engage with local and national campaigns in defence of asylum seekers. This involvement has taken a number of different forms. First, there has been research into the experience of asylum seekers and the ways in which that experience impacts on their physical and mental health, often undertaken with the support of asylum seekers' organisations (Ferguson and Barclay, 2002; Hayes and Humphries, 2004b; Humphries, 2008). Second, there have been attempts to articulate what good social work practice with asylum seekers and refugees involves. In 2006, for example, members of the trade union UNISON and the British Association of Social Workers (BASW) produced a guide for social workers in Scotland entitled *Asylum in Scotland: Child Welfare Paramount?* (Ramsden and Stevenson, 2006; see also Hayes and Humphries, 2004b). Third, conferences such as Social Work: A Profession Worth Fighting For?, held in Britain in 2006, 2007 and 2008 (to be discussed in the final chapter), have provided an opportunity for social workers to speak directly to individual asylum seekers and campaigners for their rights, such as the 'Glasgow Girls', a group of young school students who campaigned against the deportation of their school friends. Finally, at an international level, social workers and social work academics have sometimes played a prominent role within their own countries, in highlighting, for example, the plight of the 'Erased' people in Slovenia (Dedić et al, 2003) or setting up a 'People's Inquiry into Detention' in Australia to call to account the government of Malcolm Fraser for its brutal treatment of those seeking asylum in Australia's shores (Briskman et al, 2008).

Global social movements

Finally, as discussed in Chapter Two, in the past, social movements *outside* social work, like the women's movement in the 1960s and 1970s, have often had a major impact on the ideas and practices of social workers. Elsewhere, we have discussed some of the ways in which the great social movements of our own time, namely the anti-capitalist, or global justice, movement that emerged out of the protests against the World Trade Organization in Seattle in 1999, as well as the global movement against the illegal invasion of and war in Iraq in 2003, can similarly help to inform and re-energise the social work profession today (Jones et al, 2004; Ferguson and Lavalette, 2006). Specifically with reference to the anti-capitalist movement, we have suggested that it can offer three things:

■ *A global perspective* One of the great strengths of social work at its best has been its capacity to link the structural and the personal, best summed up in C. Wright Mills' notion of the sociological imagination as linking 'public issues' and 'private troubles' (Mills, 1959). It is difficult to think of any other welfare profession that shares that perspective, even if it has often been overshadowed by a narrower, more individualistic, focus in recent years. The injunction from the anti-capitalist movement to 'think global, act local' provides a fresh basis for social workers to actively make the connections between the neoliberal global agenda and their day-to-day experience as social work teachers, workers and clients, and also provides us with the basis for a new, global social work theory and practice (Bircham and Charlton, 2001).

■ *Values* There is considerable overlap between some of the core values of the anti-capitalist movement and critical social work values. Perhaps the core value statement of the movement is best summed up in the slogan 'The world is not a commodity'. As we noted in earlier chapters, much of the current unhappiness of social workers stems precisely from the fact that within neoliberal social work, everything – their professional skills, their time, their relationships with clients – *has* been turned into a commodity that can be measured and costed. Other core movement values such as justice and democracy also have a long tradition within social work, particularly its community development strand. Contact with the ideas and activities of the movement can help renew and refresh social work's value base (Callinicos, 2003; Albert, 2004).

■ *Vision* Whatever their disagreements, uniting all wings of the anti-capitalist movement is the notion that we need to construct an alternative to neoliberalism and war, that 'another world is possible'. Not a monolithic world, but rather a world of diversity, a world in which, in the words of the Zapatista leader sub-comandante Marcos, 'there is room for many worlds. A world capable of containing all the worlds' (cited in Callinicos, 2003, p 112). That vision has been discussed, debated and elaborated by tens of thousands of people over the past five years in the World Social Forums at Porto Alegre and Mumbai, and at the European Social Forums in Florence, London and Paris. As social workers, we need to be involved in these forums and debates, both to draw on the ideas and energy that they produce and also to help us construct a positive alternative vision of an engaged work.

Finally, from a Canadian perspective, Dudziak (2004, p 141) provides a nice, concrete example of how social work educators in particular are often well placed to make the links between social work and social movements:

> It began one day in theory class, while discussing oppression in different contexts. I was talking about the anti-globalization movement and the upcoming Summit of the Americas in Quebec City [a governmental conference in 2003 aimed at promoting neoliberal policies in Central and South America in particular] when one of the students spoke up and asked, 'Why don't we go?' Many reasons against the idea flashed through my mind, mostly related to keeping my job. But why not indeed! It was an opportunity for all of us to walk the talk; for me to test the boundaries between academia and activism and an opportunity for us to put some theory into practice.

She then describes how over the next two months, preparations, both practical and educational, were made and an affinity group formed made up of 21 people, mostly social work students. This group duly went to Quebec for the duration of the Summit, living together and participating both in the discussions and debates at an alternative 'People's Summit' and also in the protests outside the Summit itself. Perhaps not surprisingly, she says, the experience (which included being tear-gassed by riot police) 'was profoundly transformative for each of us in different ways. On returning home it also opened doors to further engagement on the local level' (Dudziak, 2004, p 141).

Her conclusions concern the need for social workers to reconnect the political with the social (rather than seeing social work as some 'neutral' activity, standing aloof from political conflicts and divisions); to play an active role in creating and sustaining communities; and to develop a form of practice that 'links communities in solidarity as one strategy for attending to both the global and the local' (Dudziak, 2004, pp 152-3).

Collective organisation of social workers

In the previous sections, we looked at how social workers in the 21st century might employ collective approaches in their work with service users, and also how their practice might be informed by the experience and ideas of collective movements outside social work. In this final section, we will look at the need for collective organisation of social workers themselves. The requirement for such organisation arises for two main reasons. First, for the protection of wages and conditions; however the term is defined, social workers are *workers* in the sense that, in order to live, let alone practise, they need to sell their skills to an employer. It is still the case that very few practise as independent contractors. The vast majority in the UK are employees either of local authorities or of voluntary organisations. In practice, therefore, they are subject to the same demands and constraints – for increased output, for example, or for cutting costs – as any other employee, whether in the private sector or the public sector. The dominance of managerialism over the past two decades – the belief that more efficient management, not increased resources, is the solution to most problems – has only added to these pressures, reflected in the following comments from experienced workers in Jones' study of frontline social work:

> I work much harder than I have ever worked in my life. You are expected to work at a much faster rate with no breaks. It is no wonder that so many social workers are off with stress and on long-term sick. It is appalling and it is going to get worse now we have all these league tables that are beginning to drive things. (cited in Jones, 2001, p 553)

Not surprisingly, then, a 2001 study showed that social workers in Scotland's largest council topped the council's absentee list with an average of 17 days' absence per year for each of the 4,470 staff in the department (*Scotsman*, 14 March 2001). For many social workers, as for workers generally, strong collective organisation in the form of trade unionism continues to be the most effective way of resisting management pressures for greater output.

Collective organisation is also necessary for another, rather different, reason, however. Most people who enter social work do so not simply for the money but rather because they wish to 'make a difference', whether at the level of improving the lives of individuals or working to challenge inequality and oppression. They see social work, in other words, as an *ethical* profession. The need to defend and develop that professional dimension has led in Britain and elsewhere to the creation of professional organisations, committed to promoting the views and interests of social workers.

Historically, radicals within social work, both in Britain and the US, have viewed such professionalism with suspicion, seeing it as an elitist attempt to privilege the sectional knowledge and interests of one group of workers both against other, less qualified, workers and also against people who use social work services. As Healy and Meagher (2004, p 251) comment:

> 'Classical' professionalization strategies are aimed at achieving professional closure by asserting that the expertise of a specific professional group is both exclusive to that group and essential to the performance of specific occupational duties. This strategy's institutional expression is the vehicle used by the elite professions to achieve and sustain occupational closure.

Not surprisingly, therefore, 'professionalism' was one of the main targets of the radical movement of the 1970s and is singled out for criticism in the *Case Con Manifesto*. Partly as a consequence of such criticism, but also because of its ambivalent attitude towards trade unionism and the fact that it has often been seen as an organisation of 'middle managers', BASW has never succeeded in drawing more than a minority of social workers into its ranks since its foundation in 1970 (Payne, 2002).

If, however, professionalism in the 1970s was the object of critique from the political Left, increasingly during the 1980s the main attack on professional power (or 'producer power' as it was labelled) came from the New Right, whose ideas and strategies now dominated the governing Conservative Party under Margaret Thatcher. George and Wilding (1994, p 28) neatly summarise the ideas of the New Right in the following way:

> Politicians have limited power. Consumers have less. Producer power rules. The result is services and systems geared rather to producer interests than to the public interest and the needs of service users. There are no natural corrective mechanisms which ensure service change in response to changing needs or proven deficiencies. Too many powerful people have an interest in perpetuating the status quo.

In reality, such language was little more than a smokescreen for an attack on a welfare state whose overriding weakness from a Conservative standpoint was the limited opportunities it offered to private companies to make profits. Cleverly tapping into dissatisfaction with the paternalist approaches that characterised the National Health Service in particular, the Conservatives employed the language of an apparently radical consumerism ('the empowerment of service users and carers') to drive through a 'mixed economy of care' in which, as we saw in Chapter Five, the 'extension of choice' meant greater opportunities for private business. Driving this process was a managerial approach that, as we saw in Chapter Four and in the quote earlier from Jones' respondent, systematically downgraded the knowledge, skills, discretion and professional autonomy of social workers (with one health minister, Virginia Bottomley, herself a former social worker, calling in the mid-1990s for trained social workers to be replaced by 'street-wise grannies' (Hansard, 3 June 1991).

In the very different situation of the 21st century, therefore, the 1970s' critique of professionalism needs to be revisited. One contribution to this discussion has come from Healy and Meagher (2004) who, in their discussion of what they call 'abolitionist' (that is, classical anti-professionalism) perspectives, suggest two reasons why such perspectives no longer fit.

First, they argue that deprofessionalisation is increasing gender inequality within the public sector by drawing more and more working-class and minority ethnic women into the workforce. To argue against the 'project of professionalisation' in this context, they argue, is to marginalise these women even further. If by 'the project of professionalisation' they mean here the right of these women to receive proper training, for example, or to enjoy proper wages and conditions, then their argument seems a reasonable one. However, as social care workers and day centre workers in Glasgow found in two separate disputes in 2007 and 2008, it still seems to be the case that strong trade union organisation offers the best protection against exploitation.

Their second argument is, however, a more convincing one. Despite their radical intent, they suggest that 'Abolitionist perspectives are consistent with neoliberal imperatives suggesting that professional knowledge and skill is unnecessary, perhaps even inconsistent with good social services practice' (2004, p 249). By contrast they argue:

> We contend that a poorly trained and inadequately supported human services labour force is not well placed to enact social work as a thoughtful, analytic and creative activity. Moreover, a deprofessionalized and de-skilled workforce is not in a good position to defend the interests of service users, especially when

these interests deviate from prevailing organisational and policy dictates. (2004, pp 249-50)

The argument is a strong one, and one that is likely to strike a chord with many social workers in Britain, after almost two decades during which both social work education and social work practice have been dominated by the needs and requirements of employers, and personal relationships with clients increasingly replaced by what are essentially commercial relationships with service users or 'customers'.

There is a third reason, however, not touched on by Healy and Meagher, why earlier critiques of professionalism are not always relevant to current circumstances. For it is precisely the tension between workers' notions of 'professionalism' on the one hand (in the sense of the knowledge, skills and values that they bring to the job) and the very different values and knowledge base required by currently dominant managerialist approaches on the other that is one of the main factors fuelling a new radicalism and which (in the title of a meeting of social workers in Glasgow in 2004) leads many workers to protest that 'I didn't come into social work for this!'.

Moreover, as we have argued elsewhere (Ferguson and Lavalette, 2006), that mood of resistance affects much wider layers of social workers than simply those who would see themselves as politically on the Left. The reason is simple: neoliberal social work not only challenges those who wish to employ more collective, structural approaches but also undermines the value base and the practice base of traditional social work. The domination of social work by budgets, the commodification of every aspect of the social work task, negates basic social work values, such as respect for people. So too does the moral authoritarianism which in Britain is the other face of New Labour's neoliberalism and which is reflected in the scapegoating of groups such as asylum seekers and young people who offend (Lavalette and Mooney, 1999; Butler and Drakeford, 2001). Finally, there is the fragmentation of the social work process by the domination of care management approaches that undermine the worker–client relationship, transforming it into a financial relationship, with the client reconstructed as a customer. All of these factors can create dissonance with the motivations that brought people into social work in the first place and be a potential basis for change.

For that dissatisfaction to find a voice, however, will require new, very different, notions of professionalism (and perhaps organisation) on the one hand and, as Healy and Meagher and others have suggested (see also Kimber, 2007), a 'political trade unionism' that links conditions of service issues to wider issues of social justice and equality on the other. In the final chapter, we shall discuss some recent attempts to give this widespread dissatisfaction a voice.

Questions for discussion

➲ How might a practitioner wishing to employ a more collective approach in their work with service users convince their colleagues and managers of the value of such an approach?

➲ How might social workers begin to build links with service user organisations and also wider social movements?

➲ In your own situation, what opportunities might there be for creating local forums or coalitions of social workers, service users and trade unionists to address issues of social justice?

Suggestions for further reading

➲ Callinicos, A. (2003) *An Anti-Capitalist Manifesto*, Cambridge: Polity Press. Usefully summarises the key ideas, values and strategies of the anti-capitalist movement.

➲ Humphries, B. (2008) *Social Research for Social Justice*, Basingstoke: Palgrave Macmillan. From a leading critical social work academic, explores the ways in which social research can act as a force for social change.

➲ Ledwith, M. (2005) *Community Development: A Critical Approach*, Bristol: The Policy Press. A useful attempt to demonstrate the relevance of radical perspectives (including the ideas of Paulo Freire) to community development practice today.

➲ Stepney, P. and Popple, K. (2008) *Social Work and the Community: A Critical Context for Practice*, Basingstoke: Palgrave Macmillan. Highlights the importance of the concept of community for social workers wishing to adopt a critical approach.

➲ Tew, J. (2005) *Social Perspectives in Mental Health: Developing Social Models to Understand and Work with Mental Distress*, London: Jessica Kingsley Publishers. Mainly written by professionals but gives a good flavour of the way in which service user perspectives and movements are reshaping our understanding of mental distress.

Conclusion: social work – a profession worth fighting for

Introduction: social work today

This book is based on a belief, shared by both of us, that there is a project called social work that is capable of making a positive difference to people's lives and contributing to the struggle for social justice. In fact, as the discussions in earlier chapters have shown, current versions of social work often bear little relationship to either of these goals. Yet what the book also suggests is that the *desire* for a different, more radical, social work remains strong among both workers and service users. As well as being desirable, in our view, 'another social work' is also both *necessary* and *possible*, for two main reasons. First, as we saw in earlier chapters, there is a growing dissatisfaction with neoliberal social work approaches, which have diluted social work values, sidelined relationships between social workers and service users and curtailed opportunities for critical, creative and radical practice. Second, these same neoliberal policies have resulted in the UK becoming one of the most unequal societies in the Western world. Every day, social workers are confronted with the impact of this growing inequality on people who are already our poorest and most vulnerable citizens. The combination of these two processes are fuelling a growing view that, in Cree and Davis's (2007) phrase, social work has been 'a quiet profession' for too long.

It would be wrong, of course, to see the social work profession as simply an innocent casualty of an all-powerful, neoliberal programme. As Butler and Drakeford (2001) have argued, the leadership of the profession has too often been willing to employ the rhetoric of 'empowerment' and 'user involvement' to minimise or conceal the reality of an increasingly managerial agenda. Similarly, as we saw in Chapter Two, now, as in the past, too many individual social workers are willing to collude with a controlling, authoritarian role, seeing service users as 'objects' rather than 'subjects', and viewing them 'as simultaneously weak, vulnerable and potentially dangerous' (McLaughlin, K., 2008, p vii). In addition, when under attack from a number of directions, both management and practice can become defensive. That said, it is our experience that most social workers continue to enter the profession with very different intentions and, while we would not claim that our focus group workers are necessarily representative of the profession as a whole, it was clear that they, like many others, were struggling on a daily basis to hold on to these values and to that vision. The rest of this chapter will explore how they can be helped to do so.

Creating the space

The practitioners who participated in our state and voluntary sector focus groups could still give us examples of the ways in which they tried to stay true to the ideals that brought them into the profession. In particular, there was a desire to make a positive difference to the lives of people who, for whatever reason, were struggling personally, emotionally or socially. In the state sector, social workers highlighted the importance of securing sufficient space to develop meaningful, respectful relationships with service users, based on non-judgemental attitudes and a commitment to human rights. They recognised the importance of resisting drives to further fragment and specialise social work services and of using social work values – both traditional and emancipatory – to challenge the most damaging aspects of neoliberalism. In addition, state social workers continued to believe in the importance of trade union membership and of establishing formal and informal ways in which to come together. Voluntary sector workers too did what they could to keep the needs and rights of service users at the forefront of their practice. It was apparent, however, that 'real' social work was, more often than not, just as hard for voluntary sector workers to provide as it was for their state sector colleagues. Still, person-centred and strengths-based approaches remained the preference of workers in the voluntary sector, while advocacy and, at times, campaigning work were at least options to be considered.

What we saw in all of these practitioners was a genuine commitment to social work and to service users. On the whole, focus group members did not much like the kind of social work that they were offering but felt that they did what they could in difficult circumstances to put service users first. Although little leg-room was available to them, they saw it as their responsibility – to themselves and to service users and carers – to resist in whatever small ways they could. Often this meant being overworked – because the forms still had to be completed and the targets still had to be met – but this was a necessary part of staying true to their own principles. Only by keeping the needs and rights of service users as close to centre-stage as possible could they begin to feel that they were operating as social workers rather than service brokers.

Defining radical social work

So, is it in any way possible to define radical social work for the 21st century? From the research we conducted while writing the book, it seems to us that we can identify four aspects of current radicalism in social work practice:

- radical practice as retaining a commitment to good practice;
- radical practice as 'guerrilla warfare' and small-scale resistance;
- radical practice as working alongside service users and carers;
- radical practice as collective activity and political campaigning.

We shall now consider each of these potentially radical approaches in turn.

Radical practice as retaining a commitment to good practice

Chapters Four and Five illustrate the extent to which the kind of social work on offer in agencies across the state and voluntary sectors bears, in many cases, little relation to social workers' notions of what 'real' or 'good' practice looks like. Fixated by budgets, targets, outcomes, standardised frameworks and checklists, risks and regulatory processes, social work stands little chance of remaining true to its core knowledge, skills and values. Similarly, in social work education, students on qualifying programmes are required currently to demonstrate their ability to work effectively within six key practice roles before they can be awarded their degree. The key roles are outlined within National Occupational Standards (England; TOPSS, 2002) and the Framework for Social Work Education (Scotland; Scottish Executive, 2003). As Hatton (2008, p 9) suggests, the new social work degree, introduced in 2003 on the basis of the Standards and the Framework, aims to 'enable students to work effectively as a social worker'. As academics, we share this aim, naturally, but the issue for us is that the Standards and the Framework were also introduced to 'meet the requirements laid down in the modernising agenda' (Hatton, 2008, p 9). Thus, the new degree reinforces dominant government views of social work as a 'failing profession' and of practitioners and educators as people who cannot be trusted (Woodward and Mackay, 2008). Although knowledge and skills for effective practice are essential components of the new social work degree, it is hard to see how the mechanistic approach required to achieve the Standards, which we discussed in Chapter Four, encourages the flexibility, creativity and criticality that we know to be associated with the kind of good practice workers want to offer.

Let down by the Social Services Councils – whose members ought to be resisting policy and procedural approaches that clearly fly in the face of their own definition of good social work – it has often been up to practitioners to find their own ways in which to work in the interests of service users. In small ways, however, some workers and, in our experience, many students, retain their own commitment to good practice and, in doing so, they demonstrate their radical potential.

Intellectual activity has, for some time, been recognised as an important aspect of good practice in social work (Lewis, 1982; Orcutt, 1990; Trevithick, 2005). Indeed, politicians and policy makers in the UK, given their support for an honours degree in social work, would seem to be saying the same. As suggested earlier, however, the new degree does not necessarily lend itself to the kind of intellectual work that Lewis (1982, pp 18-19) sees as so important; that which is centred on knowledge (what the social worker must know), skills (what the social worker must do) and values (who the social worker must be). Green (2006, p 251) argues that the New Labour government in the UK, despite its stated desire to raise standards across the board in social work, regularly issues 'disparaging, anti-intellectual comments about social work', as the following quotation illustrates:

> SW [social work] is a very practical job. It is about protecting people and changing their lives, not about being able to give a fluent, theoretical explanation of why they got into difficulties in the first place. (Jacqui Smith, Minister of State, cited in Green, 2006, p 251)

The social workers from the state and voluntary sectors who were interviewed for this book were clear, however, that ideas continued to form a major part of their approach to practice. Committed as they were to the critical appraisal of policy and management initiatives, their practice was based on their intellectual understanding both of the strengths and weaknesses of the work they did and of the alternative modes of practice that were within their reach. As Singh and Cowden (2006, p 8) suggest, our practitioners were, in the main, 'transformative intellectuals'; 'those whose practice is rooted in the capacity to think critically, problem solve and engage different sections of the community'. This commitment to intellectual work ought not to be considered radical – how can good practice be anything other than intellectual? It is precisely because social work has become so bureaucratic, so standardised and so watered down by the social care agenda, however, that we take time to emphasise that good social work is not simply *common sense*.

Another vital component of good practice is the building of solid relationships with service users and carers, based on respect and non-judgemental attitudes. We can remind ourselves here of something Craig, one of the state sector workers whose experiences were discussed in Chapter Four, said. Despite working in criminal justice services, where social work power is often at its most absolute, Craig was very clear about the importance of relationships:

> 'The relationship is still at the heart of it ... you build up a relationship first, you find out what really is at the heart of this person's problems and then you try to work out a shared strategy to address that.'

The centrality of relationships in social work practice is hardly a new idea. As Wilson et al (2008) suggest, relationships were at the core of the traditional, psychosocial case work models that dominated social work in the 1960s and 1970s. As might be expected, we are not recommending a return to the days of social worker as therapeutic expert. Indeed, we argue elsewhere (Chapter Seven, this volume; Ferguson, 2008, p 134) that individual responses are only one approach and that social work education and practice need to rediscover the merits of community work and group work. We do see the merits in modern relationship-based practice, however, particularly as an antidote to bureaucracy and managerialism.

The relationship-based model proposed by Wilson et al (2008, pp 7–8) seems to us to reflect exactly what some of our focus group members were telling us.

Box 8.1: Core characteristics of relationship-based practice

Relationship-based practice:

- recognises that each social work encounter is unique;
- understands that human behaviour is complex and multifaceted, that is, people are not simply rational beings but have affective – conscious and unconscious – dimensions that enrich but simultaneously complicate human relationships;
- focuses on the inseparable nature of the internal and external worlds of individuals and the importance of integrated – psychosocial – as opposed to polarised responses to social problems;
- accepts that human behaviour and the professional relationships are integral components of any professional intervention;
- places particular emphasis on the 'use of self' and the relationship as the means through which interventions are channelled.

As a social worker one of the biggest challenges you will face is being able to simultaneously focus in professional encounters on what is happening for the service user and what is happening to you. By developing this ability to understand holistically the service user's and your own responses to a specific situation you will ensure that you are acting in the service user's best interests.

Equally important to many social workers is value-based practice. Recent years have seen a watering down of the central place of values in social work. We discussed in Chapter Three just how unconcerned neoliberal politicians are with notions of equality and social justice, preferring instead the language of responsibility, individualism and, that poor relation of equality, inclusion. It comes as no surprise, then, that value-based and ethical practice has become increasingly difficult to achieve (Woodward and Mackay, 2008). That the National Occupational Standards continue to list the values that are core to effective social work practice is helpful (TOPSS, 2002, p 10). Unfortunately, the same cannot be said for the Scottish standards, which emphasise the knowledge to be gained and the outcomes to be achieved with only three mentions of 'values' in 18 pages. Sarah Banks, who has published widely on the subject of ethics and values in social work, sums up neatly just how difficult it has become for social workers to provide good, value-based practice by giving an example from the child protection arena:

> [There is now] further reorganisation of services for children and young people, more systematic inter-professional working and the use of shared information technology systems.... While they are presented as 'benign' systems for enabling welfare agencies and professionals to prevent harm and promote child welfare, there are inevitable concerns about increasing surveillance systems, invasion of privacy and infringements of professional relationships of confidentiality. (Banks, 2006, pp 145-6)

Members of the statutory and voluntary sector focus groups were adamant, however, that values remained core to their practice. More traditional values, based on 'respect' and 'empathy', were mentioned by workers but it was the need to adhere to more radical, emancipatory values that was most emphasised. This is not to suggest that traditional and emancipatory values are in any way mutually exclusive. Just as Pease and Fook (1999b, p 5) have argued that traditional skills can be used in radical ways, so too can traditional values complement more radical ones. Without respect for service users and carers, a non-judgemental take on their circumstances and an empathic understanding of their needs, there would be no claim to either a just or an anti-discriminatory practice. As it was, focus group members spoke of 'justice' (and 'injustice'), 'rights', 'discrimination' and 'oppression'. It was argued that good social work has to take account of structural inequality and that this is particularly important now precisely because so many of the recent developments in social work have anything but a 'benign' effect on staff or service users and carers.

It is this willingness to challenge the more insidious aspects of the modernisation agenda – in particular managerialism – by prioritising both relationship-based and value-based practice that can be seen as radical in the current climate. The needs and rights of service users and carers are recognised, correctly, as the cornerstone of professional practice. We suggest, however, that we need to extend our understanding of radical practice beyond this 'good practice is radical practice' paradigm. More needs to be done in practice and academic circles if radical ideas are to penetrate the mainstream.

Radical practice as 'guerrilla warfare' and small-scale resistance

> But you grow up and you calm down and
> You're working for the clampdown.
> You start wearing the blue and brown and
> You're working for the clampdown.
> So you got someone to boss around
> It makes you feel big now.
> You drift until you brutalize
> You made your first kill now.
> (© Strummer and Jones, 1979)

From the lyrics of this Clash song (which appeared in the 1979 album, *London Calling*) it becomes apparent how difficult it can be to stay in touch with radical ideas we have had when younger. As we begin to work, to earn money and to take on financial commitments, what was once important to us may become less so. In social work terms, we mention elsewhere that the profession, traditionally and currently, tends to stay quiet even though this lays every one of us connected to social work open to the accusation that we are part of the problem. In this section of the conclusion, we offer some evidence to suggest that, while the official bodies of social work – the Inspectorate, the Social Care Councils and the Institutes for Excellence – rarely criticise, publicly, new policy, management or practice initiatives, frontline practitioners and managers are resisting in small-scale but purposeful ways.

Conor is one of the state social workers who took part in the focus group for the book. He gave us a description of the ways in which he and his colleagues did what they could to subvert overly bureaucratic, managerially driven processes in the best interests of both workers and service users. In relation to written assessments and performance indicators, Conor had this to say:

> '[W]ritten assessments … are not for anybody's benefit apart from the system's. The Single Shared Assessment has been rolled out throughout [Authority X] and is certainly an example of where they've … designed a document not to [be] easily read; they've actually designed it to capture information that's needed for performance indicators – that much has been admitted by senior management. So what's happening is that there's a kind of guerrilla warfare practice developing amongst staff. There's whole swathes of these huge, long documents, about sixteen pages, just for one review – ridiculous! But people are just ignoring them and getting on in their own way and doing it in a way that's friendly to service users and useful for staff.'

While Conor and his agency colleagues practised 'guerrilla warfare', Kathryn, also a state social worker from the focus group, described herself as an "outlaw". Unwilling to turn a blind eye to unmet needs and service user distress, she and her team colleagues almost constantly "passed information back up the line to senior management". She much preferred to be a thorn in her managers' sides than to turn her back on the many disabled service users who needed her to speak with and for them. Murray, coming from a statutory youth justice service, also saw the importance of "using the systems against the system". Using the statistics that they were required by senior managers to keep in relation to young people's involvement in offending, he and some of his colleagues were able to emphasise that young people coming into contact with youth justice teams had multiple, complex personal and social needs. In Murray's words:

> 'By repeating at every management meeting … that young people who offend are just young people who have needs and who are damaged [eventually] they just invested more money in our generic childcare … so you do have room to manoeuvre … there is some hope even within that doctrine of managerialism.'

In his essential text on the establishment of the 'social work business', published in 2003, John Harris noted that social workers 'are learning to live creatively with, and at times move beyond, the constraints of the social work business, rather than being subordinated by it' (2003, p 185). We have already emphasised the radical potential within social workers who continue to offer good practice to service users and carers. Building on this, we see also attempts to practise in resistance-based ways. With words like 'agitating', 'battling' and 'challenging' being bandied about, it was apparent that the state social workers who took part in the focus groups for the book were ready for something of a struggle. Voluntary sector workers, although they echoed neither Conor's call for guerrilla warfare, nor Kathryn's preference for outlaw status, emphasised a quiet belief in resistance. For example, several fought for opportunities to 'lobby' and to 'campaign' on behalf of service users. Others considered themselves to be campaigners for the voluntary sector itself, which they saw as under threat from privatisation, the contract culture and a concerted effort by local and central government to squeeze budgets.

It seems a pity that so much professional energy has to be expended trying to undo some of the damage that has been inflicted on social work, social workers and service users and carers. It is heartening, though, to hear from experienced practitioners who do what they can to resist, albeit often at a fairly low level. Such small-scale resistance can gather momentum, however; as more people agree to take part, managers are forced to listen. As Murray's story earlier illustrates, one Scottish authority is boosting its childcare services in response to pressure brought to bear by staff within its own agency. All of our focus groups' members were as committed to good social work as they were to quietly challenging what they saw as bad social work decisions in policy, management and practice. As we note earlier, though, the social work profession, when taken as a whole, rarely speaks out against neoliberal modernisation. In some ways it is probably easier, or at least safer, to go with the flow, to avoid sticking one's neck out and to evade the label of 'difficult' or 'not being a team player'. Small-scale resistance, however, is to be celebrated in our view as, potentially, the start of something bigger. Like a commitment to good, value-based practice, however, it is not enough on its own.

Radical practice as working alongside service users and carers

Chapter Six considered the relatively recent moves in policy and practice circles to involve service users and carers in the planning, delivery and evaluation of social work services. Although a complex and contradictory process, characterised by ambiguity and inconsistency, we concluded that the meaningful involvement of service users and carers in all aspects of social work policy and practice is one of the ways in which the profession can move forward in a more radical direction. We recognised the pitfalls and that it is service users and carers, ultimately, who have most to lose when attempts to involve them are either half-hearted, tokenistic and underfunded or are not accompanied by a genuine belief in the strengths and rights of people who use services. Frances, one of the voluntary sector focus group members sums up the potential problems well:

> '[S]o what my experience of service user involvement ultimately is, is that it almost reaches a dead end. It's like we had a really good stab at it in the voluntary sector and then we'd run out of a … strategic idea of what we were offering to people … it leaves quite a lot of frustration for people [who think] that they're shaping things … but it's a glass ceiling for them.'

When it works, though, it is acknowledged that it benefits staff, users and carers: barriers are broken down and both sides learn from each other. The involvement of service users and carers in the education of student social workers is a requirement of the new social work degree. When changes are externally imposed in this way, there is always the risk that resentment will build: there remains insufficient money and time to support service user and carer involvement and there is always concern about the extent to which the agenda has been embraced by the mainstream and is politically, rather than user and carer, driven. In our experience, however, tutors, students and service users gain rather than lose in the process. For example, second-year undergraduates have opportunities to meet with users and carers to hear about their experiences of social work and to think about their own role and the power they will hold in relation to service users and carers. This is only the beginning, however, and most universities ought to fight for the space and resources to encourage and sustain the participation of service users and carers.

At the 2008 Joint Social Work Education Conference (JSWEC) in Cambridge, two university lecturers and one service user – a young woman who had spent years being looked after by the state – held a workshop on the topic of involving looked-after young people in social work education. The model used seemed to work for all concerned.

Box 8.2: Involving service users in social work education

At Birmingham University, service users are not just involved in one-off sessions with students. Rather, they are concerned with the design and delivery of a full module. The aim is to move beyond the tendency to see service users and carers as good for providing personal testimonies but not much else. The lessons that both tutors and service users learned during the module period were:

- It is important to start slowly to build up trusting relationships and understand each other's roles and perspectives (walk don't run).
- It is important to reflect throughout on what helps and what does not.
- Tutors have to be prepared to step out of their ivory tower.
- Tutors have an ongoing duty of care to service users.
- Power dynamics have to be acknowledged and dealt with.
- Preparation is needed to deal with practicalities like time, travel, money and contingency planning (cannot rely on the same service users to give up their time year after year).
- Meaningful participation requires a whole systems strategy – university culture, structures and practices have to change.

Students too were greatly appreciative as the following quotes illustrate:

'[T]he peer educators ... have stories that will dissolve your heartstrings and wry humour that will lift your spirits.'

'Having S. and R. as part of the children and families teaching group has encouraged us to continue in children and families social work, and has inspired us to improve our practice.'

Source: Richards et al (2008)

McLaughlin (2008) is most likely right to raise a cautionary point about building partnerships between service users, carers and social workers. He suggests that it is by no means apparent how service user groups – many of which are doing very well by themselves (and he cites here the Hearing Voices Network set up by and for people experiencing mental ill-health) – stand to benefit from closer alignments with social workers, who usually hold most of the cards. From our perspective, it would certainly not be in keeping with social work's commitment to value-based good practice for workers, managers or educators to impose themselves on service users or carers who had no use for them; this smacks of paternalism. Many service user organisations neither need nor want social work involvement. In addition, within neoliberal discourses, the dominant model of user involvement is a consumerist model, which often sets users *against* workers, as well as reflecting an individualist approach (personalisation), which increasingly sees people as responsible for their own welfare (Ferguson, 2007). It remains the case, though, that where practitioners are required to work with service users and carers – whether through statutory roles or voluntary support arrangements – stronger professional relationships will be built on partnership models than they will on authoritarian ones. Not every service user or carer will want to be involved in planning and evaluating social work services or in teaching student social workers. Ultimately, however, users and carers have a right to be involved at various levels and, for some, participation will increase their control over the processes to which, until fairly recently, they were often merely subjected.

Radical practice as collective activity and political campaigning

As Davis and Garrett (2004, pp 13-14) argue:

> Social workers are faced daily with contested accounts of inequality and oppression from personal, cultural and institutional sources. Service users' desolate, angry and resilient testimonies about their lives collide with, and often contradict, official accounts of the kinds of people who use social services and why.

In Chapter Two, we acknowledged not only social work's long-term concern with people living in often desperate poverty and experiencing appalling inequalities, but also its persistent inability to challenge the systemic problems behind this enduring oppression. Then, in Chapter Three, we emphasised the extent to which inequality and social polarisation has become even more entrenched as first Margaret Thatcher's Conservatives and then Blair and Brown, as New Labourites, decided to put the market first and people second. Social work cannot take responsibility for all of society's ills but, equally, in an increasingly polarised society, the profession cannot claim to seek social justice if all it does is focus on individual needs and behaviour. In Chapter Seven, we discussed some of social work's links to wider social movements – the women's and the disability movements, for example – and the influence that these connections have had on the profession in terms of its stated commitment to anti-oppressive practice and social justice. More recently, some have seen the social movements of the first decade of the 21st century, above all the anti-capitalist or global social justice movement, as well as the movement against war in Iraq, as also offering social work the chance to be part of a wider struggle against neoliberal values and priorities (Ferguson and Lavalette, 2004).

Conclusion: 'a profession worth fighting for'

For much of the past two decades, social workers in the UK have tended to suffer in silence, not least as a result of the battering that they received under the Conservative governments of the 1980s and 1990s. There are signs, however, that, at last, things are beginning to change. In recent years, a number of initiatives have been launched, often by a few individuals with very limited resources, aimed at reconnecting the profession with its core values and visions. Here, we give just a few examples. The Social Work and Health Inequalities Network has been tireless in highlighting the ways in which health inequalities shape and distort the lives of people who use social work services, and is having an increasing impact on the policies and practice of the profession at a global level. Similarly, the Shaping Our Lives National Service User Network is bringing the *collective* voice of service users to bear on government and on the health and social work professions. For the past few years, a biennial conference has taken place in Nottingham under the title Affirming Our Values in Social Work with up to 2,000, social work practitioners, managers, students and service users turning up to listen to some of the profession's best-known radicals, such as Bob Holman and Peter Beresford.

Finally, both of us have been actively involved in building the Social Work Action Network (SWAN), a loose coalition of workers, academics and service users based on the Social Work Manifesto that was launched in 2004 (Jones et al, 2004). SWAN's main activity to date has been the organisation of a series of annual conferences entitled Social Work: A Profession Worth Fighting For?. Since 2006, these conferences have addressed a wide range of issues including social work and asylum seekers, the demonisation of young people, the impact of managerialism, and social work and women's oppression today. Following its 2008 conference at Liverpool Hope University, SWAN groups are now being established in most parts of the UK with a view to campaigning around local issues. At the same time, the involvement of international delegates in these conferences means that similar groups are also being established in several other countries, including Greece, India and Japan.

These are small beginnings. What they represent, however, is a real attempt to challenge the market-driven agenda of the past two decades, which has been so destructive both for those who work in social work and for those on the receiving end of social work services. They are the green shoots of a new, engaged practice that can make a positive difference to people's lives. Finally, in their commitment to the values of social justice and opposition to all forms of oppression, they represent the welcome reappearance of a radical tradition within social work that has been silent for far too long.

References

Abbott, P. and Wallace, C. (1997) *An Introduction to Sociology: Feminist Perspectives* (2nd edn), London: Routledge.

Action for Advocacy (2002) *The Advocacy Charter*, London: Action for Advocacy.

Adams, R. (2002) 'Social work processes', in R. Adams, L. Dominelli and M. Payne (eds) *Social Work: Themes, Issues and Critical Debates* (2nd edn), Basingstoke: Palgrave/Open University Press.

Adams, R., Dominelli, L. and Payne, M. (eds) (2002) *Social Work: Themes, Issues and Critical Debates*, Basingstoke: Palgrave/Open University Press.

Albert, M. (2004) *Parecon: Life after Capitalism*, London: Verso.

Alinsky, S. (1971) *Rules for Radicals*, New York, NY: Vintage Books.

Allan, J., Pease, B. and Briskman, L. (2003) *Critical Social Work: An Introduction to Theories and Practices*, Australia: Allen and Unwin.

Aspis, S. (1997) 'Self-advocacy for people with learning difficulties: does it have a future?', *Disability and Society*, 12 (4), 647-58.

Attlee, C. (1920) *The Social Worker*, London: Heinemann.

Aubrey, C. and Dahl, S. (2005) 'Children's voices: the views of vulnerable children on their service providers and the relevance of services they receive', *British Journal of Social* Work, 36 (1), 21-39.

Audit Commission (2002) *Recruitment and Retention: A Public Service Workforce for the 21st Century*, London: The Stationery Office.

Bailey, R. and Brake, M. (eds) (1975) *Radical Social Work*, London: Edward Arnold.

Banks, S. (2006) *Ethics and Values in Social Work* (3rd edn), Basingstoke: Palgrave Macmillan.

Barclay, P. (1982) *Social Workers: Their Role and Tasks* (the Barclay Report), London: Bedford Square Press.

Barnes, M. and Shardlow, P. (1996) 'Identity crisis: mental health user groups and the "problem" of identity', in C. Barnes and G. Mercer (eds) *Exploring the Divide*, Leeds: The Disability Press.

Barr, A. (1991) *Practising Community Development: Experience in Strathclyde*, London: Community Development Foundation.

Barry, M. (2006) 'Dispensing with justice? Young people's views of the criminal justice system', in K. Gorman, M. Gregory, M. Hayles and N. Parton (eds) *Constructive Work with Offenders*, London: Jessica Kingsley Publishers.

Barry, M. (2007) *Effective Approaches to Risk Assessment in Social Work: An International Literature Review*, Edinburgh: Scottish Executive.

Beck, U. (2000) *What is Globalization?*, Cambridge: Polity Press.

Beresford, P. (2005) 'Social approaches to madness and distress: user approaches and user knowledges', in J. Tew (ed) *Social Perspectives in Mental Health: Developing Social Models to Understand and Work with Mental Distress*, London: Jessica Kingsley Publishers.

Beresford, P. (2007) *The Changing Roles and Tasks of Social Work from Service Users' Perspectives: A Literature Informed Discussion Paper*, London: Shaping Our Lives National User Network.

Beresford, P. and Croft, S. (2004) 'Service users and practitioners reunited: the key component for social work reform', *British Journal of Social Work*, 34 (1), 53-68.

Beresford, P., Adshead, L. and Croft, S. (2007) *Palliative Care, Social Work and Service Users: Making Life Possible*, London: Jessica Kingsley Publishers.

Bernard, C. (2002) 'Giving voice to experiences: parental mistreatment of black children in the context of societal racism', *Child and Family Social Work*, 7 (4), 239-53.

Bircham, E. and Charlton, J. (2001) *Anti-Capitalism: A Guide to the Movement*, London: Bookmarks.

Black, C. (2008) *Working for a healthier tomorrow: Dame Carol Black's Review of the health of Britain's working population*, London: The Stationery Office.

Bourdieu, P. (1998) *Acts of Resistance: Against the New Myths of Our Time*, Cambridge: Polity Press.

Branfield, F. and Beresford, P. with Andrews, E.J., Chambers, P., Staddon, P., Wise, G. and Williams-Findlay, B. (2006) *Making User Involvement Work: Supporting Service User Networking and Knowledge*, York: Joseph Rowntree Foundation.

Briskman, L., Latham, S. and Goddard, C. (2008) *Human Rights Overboard: Seeking Asylum in Australia under the Howard Government*, Carlton, Australia: Scribe Publications.

Brown, C. (2004) 'Social work as intervention: the deconstruction of individuals as a means of gaining a legislative perspective to remain in the United Kingdom', in D. Hayes and B. Humphries (eds) *Social Work, Immigration and Asylum*, London: Jessica Kingsley Publishers.

Brown, G. (2004) Keynote speech to the National Council for Voluntary Organisations' Annual Conference (www.ncvo-vol.org.uk/press/speeches/index.asp?id=2460).

Bryant, B. and Bryant, R. (1982) *Change and Conflict: A Study of Community Work in Glasgow*, Aberdeen: Aberdeen University Press.

Burgess, H. (2004) 'Redesigning the curriculum for social work education: complexity, conformity, chaos, creativity, collaboration?', *Social Work Education*, 23 (2), 163-83.

Butler, I. and Drakeford, M. (2001) 'Which Blair project? Communitarianism, social authoritarianism and social work', *Journal of Social Work*, 1 (1), 7–19.

Butler, I. and Pugh, R. (2004) 'The politics of social work research', in R. Lovelock, K. Lyons and J. Powell (eds) *Reflecting on Social Work: Discipline and Profession*, Aldershot: Ashgate.

Callinicos, A. (2001) *Against the Third Way*, Cambridge: Polity Press.

Callinicos, A. (2003) *An Anti-Capitalist Manifesto*, Cambridge: Polity Press.

Campbell, J. (1997) '"Growing pains" disability politics: the journal explained and described', in L. Barton and M. Oliver (eds) *Disability Studies: Past, Present and Future*, Leeds: The Disability Press.

Campbell, J. and Oliver, M. (1996) *Disability Politics: Understanding our Past, Changing our Future*, London: Routledge.

Campbell, P. (1996) 'The history of the user movement in the United Kingdom', in T. Heller, J. Reynolds, R. Gomm, R. Muston and S. Pattison (eds) *Mental Health Matters: A Reader*, Basingstoke: Macmillan.

Carey, M. (2008) 'Everything must go? The privatization of state social work', *British Journal of Social Work*, 38 (5), 918–35.

Carniol, B. (2005) *Case Critical: Social Services & Social Justice in Canada* (5th edn), Canada: Between the Lines Productions.

Carvel, J. (2007) 'Public service targets to be scrapped', *The Guardian*, 18 July.

Cemlyn, S. and Briskman, L. (2003) 'Asylum, children's rights and social work', *Child and Family Social Work*, 8, 163–78.

Charles, M. with Wilton, J. (2004) 'Creativity and constraint in child welfare', in M. Lymbery and S. Butler (eds) *Social Work Ideals and Practice Realities*, Basingstoke: Palgrave Macmillan.

Charlton, J. (2000) 'Class struggle and the origins of welfare state reform', in G. Mooney and M. Lavalette (eds) *Class Struggle and Social Welfare*, London: Routledge.

Clarke, J. (2004) 'Dissolving the public realm? The logics and limits of neo-liberalism', *Journal of Social Policy*, 33 (1), 27–48.

Cochrane, A. and Pain, K. (2004) 'A globalizing society?', in D. Held (ed) *A Globalizing World? Culture, Economics, Politics* (2nd edn), London: Routledge/Open University Press.

Collett, J. (2004) 'Immigration is a social work issue', in D. Hayes and B. Humphries (eds) *Social Work, Immigration and Asylum*, London: Jessica Kingsley Publishers.

Corby, B. (2006) *Child Abuse: Towards a Knowledge Base* (3rd edn), Maidenhead: Open University Press/McGraw Hill.

Corrigan, P. and Leonard, P. (1978) *Social Work under Capitalism: A Marxist Approach*, London: Macmillan.

Cowden, S. and Singh, G. (2007) 'The "user": friend, foe or fetish? A critical exploration of user involvement in health and social care', *Critical Social Policy*, 27 (5), 5-23.

Cree, V.E. and Cavanagh, K. (1996) 'Men, masculinism and social work', in K. Cavanagh and V.E. Cree (eds) *Working with Men: Feminism and Social Work*, London: Routledge.

Cree, V.E. and Davis, A. (2007) *Social Work: Voices from the Inside*, London: Routledge.

Cretney, S. (2006) *Same-Sex Relationships: From 'Odious Crime' to 'Gay Marriage'*, Oxford: Oxford University Press.

Crossley, N. (1999) 'Fish, field, habitus and madness: the first wave mental health users movement in Great Britain', *British Journal of Sociology*, 50 (4), 647-70.

CSCI (Commission for Social Care Inspection) (2007a) *The State of Social Care in England, 2005/6: Executive Summary*, London: CSCI.

CSCI (2007b) Press Release, 10 January, London: CSCI.

Cunningham, I. and James, P. (2007) *False Economy? The Costs of Contracting and Insecurity in the Voluntary Sector*, London: UNISON.

Curran, G. (2006) *21st Century Dissent: Anarchism, Anti-Globalization and Environmentalism*, Basingstoke: Palgrave Macmillan.

CWDC (Children's Workforce Development Council) (2007) *Common Assessment Framework for Children and Young People: Practitioners' Guide*, Leeds: CWDC.

Dalrymple, J. (2003) 'Professional advocacy as a force for resistance in child welfare', *British Journal of Social Work*, 33 (8), 1043-62.

Dalrymple, J. (2004) 'Constructions of child and youth advocacy: emerging issues in advocacy practice', *Children and Society*, 19 (1), 3-15.

Davies, N. (1998) *Dark Heart: The Shocking Truth about Hidden Britain*, London: Vintage.

Davies, S. (2006) *Third Sector Provision of Employment-Related Services*, London: Public and Commercial Services Union.

Davis, A. and Garrett, P.M. (2004) 'Progressive practice for tough times: social work, poverty and division in the twenty-first century', in M. Lymbery and S. Butler (eds) *Social Work Ideals and Practice Realities*, Basingstoke: Macmillan.

DCSF (Department for Children, Schools and Families) (2007) *Care Matters: Transforming the Lives of Children and Young People in Care*, Nottingham: DCSF Publications.

Dedić, J., Jalušić, V. and Zorn, J. (2003) *The Erased: Organized Innocence and the Politics of Exclusion*, Ljubljana, Slovenia: Peace Institute.

DfES (Department for Education and Skills) (2004) *Every Child Matters: Change for Children*, London: DfES.

DH (Department of Health) (2000) *Framework for the Assessment of Children in Need and their Families,* London: DH.

DH (2002a) *Requirements for Social Work Training,* London: DH.

DH (2002b) *National Standards for the Provision of Children's Advocacy Services,* London: DH.

DH/DfES (Department of Health/Department for Education and Skills) (2006) *Options for Excellence: Building the Social Care Workforce of the Future,* London: DH/DfES.

Docherty, A., Harkness, E., Eardley, M., Townson, L. and Chapman, R. (2006) 'What they want – yes, but what we want – bugger us!', in D. Mitchell, R. Traustadúttir, R. Chapman, L. Townson, N. Ingham and S. Ledger (eds) *Exploring Experiences of Advocacy by People with Learning Disabilities,* London: Jessica Kingsley Publishers.

Doel, M. and Best, L. (2008) *Experiencing Social Work, Learning from Service Users,* London: Sage Publications.

Dominelli, L. (2002a) *Feminist Social Work Theory and Practice,* Basingstoke: Palgrave.

Dominelli, L. (2002b) 'Anti-oppressive practice in context', in R. Adams, L. Dominelli and M. Payne (eds) *Social Work: Themes, Issues and Critical Debates,* Basingstoke: Palgrave/Open University Press.

Dominelli, L. (2002c) 'Deprofessionalizing social work: anti-oppressive practice, competencies and postmodernism', *British Journal of Social Work,* 26 (2), 153-75.

Donnellan, H. and Jack, G. (2008) 'NQSWs: the first year', *Community Care,* 28 February.

Drakeford, M. (2006) 'Ownership, regulation and the public interest: the case of residential care for older people', *Critical Social Policy,* 26 (4), 932-44.

Dudziak, S. (2004) 'Educating for justice: challenges and openings in the context of globalisation', in I. Ferguson, M. Lavalette and E. Whitmore (eds) *Globalisation, Global Justice and Social Work,* London: Routledge.

Dustin, D. (2007) *The McDonaldization of Social Work,* Aldershot: Ashgate.

DWP (Department for Work and Pensions) (2007a) *New Measures to Lift Thousands More Children Out of Poverty Announced,* Press Release, 27 March, London: DWP.

DWP (2007b) *Working for Children,* London: DWP.

Eadie, T. and Lymbery, M. (2007) 'Promoting creative practice through social work education', *Social Work Education,* 26 (7), 670-83.

Eborall, C. and Garmeson, K. (2001) *Desk Research on Recruitment and Retention in Social Care and Social Work,* London: Business and Industrial Market Research.

Elliott, L. and Atkinson, D. (2008) *The Gods that Failed: How Blind Faith in Markets has Cost Us Our Future,* London: The Bodley Head.

Evans, S., Huxley, P., Gately, C., Webber, M., Mears, A., Pahak, S., Medina, J., Kendall, T. and Katona, C. (2006) 'Mental health, burnout and job satisfaction among mental health social workers in England and Wales', *British Journal of Psychiatry*, 188 (1), 75-80.

Farnsworth, K. (2006) 'Capital to the rescue? New Labour's business solutions to old welfare problems', *Critical Social Policy*, 26 (4), 817-42.

Ferguson, I. (2007) 'Increasing user choice or privatizing risk? The antinomies of personalization', *British Journal of Social Work*, 37 (3), 387-403.

Ferguson, I. (2008) *Reclaiming Social Work: Challenging Neo-Liberalism and Promoting Social Justice*, London: Sage Publications.

Ferguson, I. and Barclay, A. (2002) *Seeking Peace of Mind: The Mental Health Needs of Asylum Seekers in Glasgow*, Stirling: University of Stirling (www.dass.stir.ac.uk).

Ferguson, I. and Lavalette, M. (2004) 'Beyond power discourse: alienation, and social work', *British Journal of Social Work*, 34 (3), 297-312.

Ferguson, I. and Lavalette, M. (2006) 'Globalization and global justice: towards a social work of resistance', *International Social Work*, 49 (3), 309-18.

Ferguson, I. and Lavalette, M. (eds) (2007a) *International Social Work and the Radical Tradition*, London: Venture Press.

Ferguson, I. and Lavalette, M. (2007b) 'The social worker as agitator: the radical kernel of British Social Work', in M. Lavalette and I. Ferguson (eds) *International Social Work and the Radical Tradition*, London: Venture Press.

Ferguson, I., Lavalette, M. and Mooney, G. (2002) *Rethinking Welfare: A Critical Perspective*, London: Sage Publications.

Flaherty, J., Veit-Wilson, J. and Dornan, P. (2004) *Poverty: The Facts* (5th edn), London: Child Poverty Action Group.

Fook, J. (1993) *Radical Casework: A Theory of Practice*, Sydney: Allen and Unwin.

Fook, J. and Askeland, G.A. (2007) 'Challenges of critical reflection: "nothing ventured, nothing gained"', *Social Work Education*, 26 (5), 520-33.

Forbat, L. and Atkinson, D. (2005) 'Advocacy in practice: the troubled position of advocates in adult services', *British Journal of Social Work*, 35 (3), 321-35.

Forbes, J. and Sashidharan, S.P. (1997) 'User involvement in services – incorporation or challenge', *British Journal of Social Work*, 27 (4), 481-98.

Franklin, A. and Sloper, P. (2004) *Participation of Disabled Children and Young People in Decision-Making within Social Services Departments in England*, York: Social Policy Research Unit, University of York.

Fraser, H. and Briskman, L. (2004) 'Through the eye of a needle: the challenge of getting justice in Australia if you're indigenous or seeking asylum', in I. Ferguson, M. Lavalette and E. Whitmore (eds) *Globalisation, Global Justice and Social Work*, London: Routledge.

Freire, P. (1996) *Pedagogy of the Oppressed* (2nd edn) London: Penguin.

Freud, D. (2007) *Reducing Dependency, Increasing Opportunity: Options for the Future of Welfare to Work. An Independent Report to the Department for Work and Pensions*, Leeds: Corporate Document Services.

Friedman, M. (1962 [1982]) *Capitalism and Freedom*, Chicago, IL: University of Chicago Press.

Fyfe, N.R. (2005) 'Making Space for "Neo-communitarianism"? The Third Sector, State and Civil Society in the UK', *Antipode*, 37(3), 536-57.

Garrett, P.M. (2003) *Remaking Social Work with Children and Families: A Critical Discussion on the 'Modernisation' of Social Care*, London: Routledge.

George, V. and Wilding, P. (1994) *Welfare and Ideology*, London: Harvester/Wheatsheaf.

Giddens, A. (1998) *The Third Way: The Renewal of Social Democracy*, Cambridge: Polity Press.

Giddens, A. (2000) *The Third Way and its Critics*, Cambridge: Polity Press.

Gilbert, N. and Tang, K.L. (1995) 'The United States', in N. Johnson (ed) *Private Markets in Health and Welfare: An International Perspective*, Oxford: Berg.

Glasby, J. (2005) 'The future of adult social care: lessons from previous reforms', *Research, Policy and Planning*, 23 (2), 61-70.

Glasby, J. and Beresford, P. (2006) 'Commentary and issues: who knows best? Evidence-based practice and the service user contribution', *Critical Social Policy*, 26 (1), 268-84.

Glyn, A. (2006) *Capitalism Unleashed*, Oxford: Oxford University Press.

Goldson, B. (2002) 'New Labour, social justice and children: political calculation and the deserving–undeserving schism', *British Journal of Social Work*, 32 (6), 683-95.

Goldson, B. and Muncie, J. (2006) 'Critical anatomy: towards a principled youth justice', in B. Goldson and J. Muncie (eds) *Youth Crime and Justice*, London: Sage Publications.

Gordon, D. (2000) 'Inequalities in income, wealth and standard of living in Britain', in C. Pantanzis and D. Gordon (eds) *Tackling Inequalities: Where Are We Now and What Can Be Done?*, Bristol: The Policy Press.

Gorman, K., O'Byrne, P. and Parton, N. (2006) 'Constructive work with offenders: setting the scene', in K. Gorman, M. Gregory, M. Hayles and N. Parton (eds) *Constructive Work with Offenders*, London: Jessica Kingsley Publishers.

Graham, M. (2007) *Black Issues in Social Work and Social Care*, Bristol: The Policy Press.

Grassi, E. and Alayón, N. (2005) 'Neo-liberalism in Argentina: social policy, welfare and the conditions for the development of social work', in I. Ferguson, M. Lavalette and E. Whitmore (eds) *Globalisation, Global Justice and Social Work*, London: Routledge.

Green, L.C. (2006) 'Pariah profession, debased discipline? An analysis of social work's low academic status and the possibilities of change', *Social Work Education*, 25 (3), 245-64.

Griffiths, R. (1988) *Community Care: Agenda for Action: A Report to the Secretary of State for Social Services by Sir Roy Griffiths*, London: HMSO.

GSCC (General Social Care Council) (2002) *Codes of Practice for Social Care Workers and Employers*, London: GSCC.

GSCC (2008) 'How we consulted you', from Codes of Practice web pages (www.gscc.org.uk/codes/How+we+consulted+you).

Guardian Society (2008) 'Unions find more losers than winners', 20 February.

Hanmer, J. and Statham, D. (1988) *Women and Social Work: Towards a Women-Centred Practice*, Basingstoke: Macmillan Education.

Harman, C. (2008) 'Theorising neoliberalism', *Internatioanl Socialism*, 117, 87-121.

Harris, J. (2003) *The Social Work Business*, London: Sage Publications.

Harrison, R. (2000) *The Life and Times of Sydney and Beatrice Webb 1858-1905: The Formative Years*, London: Palgrave Macmillan.

Harvey, D. (2005) *A Brief History of Neoliberalism*, Oxford: Oxford University Press.

Hatton, K. (2008) *New Directions in Social Work Practice*, Exeter: Learning Matters.

Hayek, F.A. (1949) *Individualism and Economic Order*, London: Routledge and Kegan Paul.

Hayek, F.A. (1960) *The Constitution of Liberty*, London: Routledge and Kegan Paul.

Hayes, D. and Humphries, B. (2004a) 'Conclusion', in D. Hayes and B. Humphries (eds) *Social Work, Immigration and Asylum: Debates, Dilemmas and Ethical issues for Social Work and Social Care*, London: Jessica Kingsley Publishers.

Hayes, D. and Humphries, B. (eds) (2004b) *Social Work, Immigration and Asylum: Debates, Dilemmas and Ethical issues for Social Work and Social Care*, London: Jessica Kingsley Publishers.

Healy, K. (2005) *Social Work Theories in Context: Creating Frameworks for Practice*, Basingstoke: Macmillan.

Healy, K. and Meagher, G. (2004) 'The reprofessionalization of social work: collaborative approaches for achieving professional recognition', *British Journal of Social Work*, 34 (2), 243-60.

Hedderman, C. and Hough, M. (2004) 'Getting tough or being effective: what matters?', in G. Mair (ed) *What Matters in Probation*, Cullompton: Willan.

Henderson, R. and Pochin, M. (2001) *A Right Result? Advocacy, Justice and Empowerment*, Bristol: The Policy Press.

Higham, P. (2006) *Social Work: Introducing Professional Practice*, London: Sage Publications.

Van Heugten, K. and Daniels, K. (2001) 'Social Workers who Move into Private Practice: The Impact of the Socio-Economic Context', *British Journal of Social Work*, 31, 739-55.

Hodge, S. (2005) 'Participation, discourse and power: a case study in service user involvement', *Critical Social Policy*, 25 (2), 164-79.

Holman, B. (1998) *Faith in the Poor*, London: Lion Hudson.

Hope, P. (2007) 'The role of the third sector in transforming services', Speech to the ModernGov Conference, 30 October, London: Cabinet Office.

Horner, N. (2006) *What is Social Work? Context and Perspectives* (2nd edn), Exeter: Learning Matters.

Hoy, J., Cautrels, D. and Goodley, D. with Huddersfield People First (2006) 'The life of a group and a personal story: experiences from Huddersfield People First', in D. Mitchell, R. Traustadóttir, R. Chapman, L. Townson, N. Ingham and S. Ledger (eds) *Exploring Experiences of Advocacy by People with Learning Disabilities*, London: Jessica Kingsley Publishers.

Humm, M. (1992) *Feminisms: A Reader*, Hemel Hempstead: Harvester Wheatsheaf.

Humphries, B. (2004a) 'Refugees, asylum seekers, welfare and social work', in D. Hayes and B. Humphries (eds) *Social Work, Immigration and Asylum*, London: Jessica Kingsley Publishers.

Humphries, B. (2004b) 'An unacceptable role for social work: implementing immigration policy', *British Journal of Social Work*, 34 (1), 93-107.

Humphries, B. (2008) *Social Research for Social Justice*, Basingstoke: Palgrave Macmillan.

IFSW/IASSW (International Federation of Social Workers/International Association of Schools of Social Work) (2000) *The Definition of Social Work*, Berne: IFSW.

Institute for Applied Health and Social Policy (2002) *Service User Focus Groups on the Reform of Social Work Education and Training*, London: Department of Health.

IRISS (Institute for Research and Innovation in Social Services) (2008) *The Golden Bridge: Child Migration from Scotland to Canada 1869-1939*, online exhibition, Dundee: IRISS (www.iriss.ac.uk/goldenbridge).

Johnson, N. (ed) (1995a) *Private Markets in Health and Welfare: An International Perspective*, Oxford: Berg.

Johnson, N. (1995b) 'The United Kingdom', in N. Johnson (ed) *Private Markets in Health and Welfare: An International Perspective*, Oxford: Berg.

Jones, C. (1983) *State Social Work and the Working Class*, London: Routledge and Kegan Paul.

Jones, C. (1999) 'Social work: regulation and managerialism', in M. Hexworthy and S. Halford (eds) *Professionals and the New Managerialism in the Public Sector*, Buckingham: Open University Press.

Jones, C. (2001) 'Voices from the front line: state social workers and New Labour', *British Journal of Social Work*, 31 (4), 547-62.

Jones, C. (2002a) 'Social work and society', in R. Adams, L. Dominelli and M. Payne (eds) *Social Work: Themes, Issues and Critical Debates* (2nd edn), London: Palgrave Macmillan.

Jones, C. (2002b) 'Children, class and the threatening state', in B. Goldson, M. Lavalette and J. McKechnie (eds) *Children, Welfare and the State*, London: Sage Publications.

Jones, C. (2005) 'The neo-liberal assault: voices from the front line of British state social work', in I. Ferguson, M. Lavalette and E. Whitmore (eds) *Globalisation, Global Justice and Social Work*, London: Routledge.

Jones, C. (2007) 'What is to be done?', in M. Lavalette and I. Ferguson (eds) *International Social Work and the Radical Tradition*, London: Venture Press.

Jones, C. and Novak, T. (1993) 'Social work today', *British Journal of Social Work*, 23 (3), 195-212.

Jones, C., Ferguson, I., Lavalette, M. and Penketh, L. (2004) *Social Work and Social Justice: A Manifesto for a New Engaged Practice*, Liverpool: University of Liverpool (www.liv.ac.uk/ssp/Social_Work_Manifesto.html).

Jordan, B. (2001) 'Tough love: social work, social exclusion and the Third Way', *British Journal of Social Work*, 31 (4), 527-46.

Jordan, B. (2007) *Social Work and Well-Being*, Lyme-Regis: Russell House.

Jordan, B. with Jordan, C. (2001) *Social Work and the Third Way: Tough Love as Social Policy*, London: Sage Publications.

JRF (Joseph Rowntree Foundation) (2006) *Monitoring Poverty and Social Exclusion in Scotland, 2006*, London: JRF.

JRF (2007) *Poverty, Wealth and Place in Britain, 1968-2005*, London: JRF.

Kelly, B. and Prokhovnik, R. (2004) 'Economic globalization?', in D. Held (ed) *A Globalizing World? Culture, Economics, Politics* (2nd edn), London: Routledge/Open University Press.

Kilbrandon, Lord (1964) *Report of the Committee on Children and Young Persons, Scotland*, Cmnd 2306, Edinburgh: HMSO.

Kimber, C. (2007) 'The politics of the post strike', *Socialist Review*, 319, November, online version (www.socialistreview.org.uk).

Knapp, M., Hardy, B. and Forder, J. (2001) 'Commissioning for quality: ten years of social care markets in England', *Journal of Social Policy*, 30 (2), 283-306.

Kohli, R. (2007) *Social Work with Unaccompanied Asylum Seeking Children*, Basingstoke: Palgrave Macmillan.

Kurlansky, M. (2004) *1968: The Year that Rocked the World*, London: Jonathan Cape.

Labour Party (2005) *The Labour Party Manifesto 2005*, London: Labour Party.

Langan, M. (1992) 'Women and social work in the 1990s', in M. Langan and L. Day (eds) *Women, Oppression & Social Work*, London: Routledge.

Langan, M. (2002) 'The legacy of radical social work', in R. Adams, L. Dominelli and M. Payne (eds) *Social Work: Themes, Issues and Critical Debates*, London: Palgrave/Open University Press.

Langan, M. and Lee, P. (eds) (1989) *Radical Social Work Today*, London: Unwin Hyman.

Lansley, S. (2006) *Rich Britain: The Rise and Rise of the New Super-Wealthy*, London: Politico's.

Lavalette, M. and Ferguson, I. (eds) (2007) *International Social Work and the Radical Tradition*, London: Venture Press.

Lavalette, M. and Mooney, G. (1999) 'New Labour, new moralism: the welfare politics and ideology of New Labour under Blair', *International Socialism*, 85, 27-47.

Leadbetter, D. (2004) *Personalisation through Participation: A New Script for Public Services*, London: Demos.

Leadbetter, D. and Lownsbrough, H. (2005) *Personalisation and Participation: The Future of Social Care in Scotland*, London: Demos.

Ledwith, M. (2005) *Community Development: A Critical Approach*, Bristol: The Policy Press.

Leonard, P. (1997) *Postmodern Welfare: Reconstructing an Emancipatory Project*, London: Sage Publications.

Levin, E. (2004) *Involving Service Users and Carers in Social Work Education*, London: Social Care Institute for Excellence.

Lewis, H. (1982) *The Intellectual Base of Social Work Practice: Tools for Thought in a Helping Profession*, London: Routledge.

Lewis, J. (1995) *The Voluntary Sector, the State and Social Work in Britain*, Aldershot: Edward Elgar.

Lister, R. with Smith, N., Middleton, S. and Cox, L. (2005) 'Young people and citizenship', in M. Barry (ed) *Youth Policy and Social Inclusion*, Abingdon: Routledge.

Little, M. (2008) 'Unions find more losers than winners', *The Guardian*, 20 February.

Lymbery, M. (2001) 'Social work at the crossroads', *British Journal of Social Work*, 31 (3), 369-84.

Lymbery, M. (2003) 'Negotiating the contradictions between competence and creativity in social work education', *Journal of Social Work*, 3 (1), 99-117.

Lymbery, M. (2004) 'Managerialism and care management practice with older people', in M. Lymbery and S. Butler (eds) *Social Work Ideals and Practice Realities*, Basingstoke: Palgrave Macmillan.

Lymbery, A. and Butler, S. (eds) (2004) *Social Work Ideals and Practice Realities*, Basingstoke: Palgrave Macmillan.

MacDonald, R. and Marsh, J. (2005) *Disconnected Youth: Growing Up in Britain's Poor Neighbourhoods*, Basingstoke: Palgrave Macmillan.

Mackay, K. and Woodward, R. (2008) 'New degree, new social work, new values: the dangers of standardised approaches to education', Paper presented at Social Work: A Profession Worth Fighting For?, 3rd annual conference, Liverpool Hope University, 13 September.

Marshall T.H. (1981) *The Right to Welfare and Other Essays*, London: Heinemann.

Martinson, R. (1974) 'What works? Questions and answers about prison reform', *The Public Interest*, 10, 22-54.

Maslach, C. and Leiter, M.P. (1997) *The Truth about Burnout: How Organizations Cause Personal Stress and What to Do About It*, San Francisco, CA: Jossey-Bass.

Maslach, C., Schaufeli, W.B. and Leiter, M.P. (2001) 'Job burnout', *Annual Review of Psychology*, vol 52, pp 397–422.

Mayer, J.E. and Timms, N. (1970) *The Client Speaks: Working-Class Impressions of Casework*, London: Routledge and Kegan Paul.

Mayo, M. (1994) *Communities and Caring: The Mixed Economy of Welfare*, Basingstoke: Palgrave Macmillan.

McAra, L. (2006) 'Welfare in crisis? Key developments in Scottish youth justice', in J. Muncie and B. Goldson (eds) *Comparative Youth Justice*, London: Sage Publications.

McDonald, A., Postle, K. and Dawson, C. (2007) 'Barriers to retaining and using professional knowledge in local authority social work practice with adults in the UK', *British Journal of Social Work*, Advance Access, published 25 April (http://bjsw.oxfordjournals.org/cgi/reprint/bcm042v1).

McDonald, C. (2006) *Challenging Social Work: The Context of Practice*, London: Palgrave.

McGourty, R.F. and Chasnoff, I.J. (2003) *Power Beyond Measure*, Chicago, Ill: NTI Publishing.

McKendrick, J., Mooney, J., Dickie, J. and Kelly, P. (eds) (2007) *Poverty in Scotland 2007*, London: Child Poverty Action Group.

McLaughlin, E. and Muncie, J. (1993) 'Juvenile delinquency', in R. Dallos and E. McLaughlin (eds) *Social Problems and the Family*, London: Sage Publications.

McLaughlin, H. (2008) 'What's in a name: "client", "patient", "customer", "consumer", "expert by experience", "service user" – what's next?', *British Journal of Social Work*, Advance Access, published 21 February (http://bjsw.oxfordjournals.org/cgi/reprint/bcm155v1).

McLaughlin, K. (2007) 'Regulation and risk in social work: the General Social Care Council and the Social Care Register in context', *British Journal of Social Work*, 37 (7), 1263-77.

McLaughlin, K. (2008) *Social Work, Politics and Society: From Radicalism to Orthodoxy*, Bristol: The Policy Press.

McNay, M. (1992) 'Social work and power relations: towards a framework for an integrated practice', in M. Langan and L. Day (eds) *Women, Oppression & Social Work*, London: Routledge.

McNeill, F., Batchelor, S., Burnett, R. and Knox, J. (2005) *21st Century Social Work: Reducing Re-Offending: Key Practice Skills*, Edinburgh: Scottish Executive.

Midgley, J. (2001) 'Issues in international social work', *Journal of Social Work*, 1 (1), 21-35.

Miller, C. (2004) *Producing Welfare*, Basingstoke: Palgrave Macmillan.

Miller, M. and Corby, B. (2006) 'The *Framework for the Assessment of Children in Need and their Families* – a basis for a "therapeutic" encounter?', *British Journal of Social Work*, 36 (6), 887-99.

Mills, C.W. (1943) 'The professional ideology of social pathologists', *The American Journal of Sociology*, 49 (2), 165-80.

Mills, C.W. (1959) *The Sociological Imagination*, Oxford: Oxford University Press.

Monbiot, G. (2007) 'How did we get into this mess?', *The Guardian*, 28 August.

Mooney, G. (1998) '"Remoralizing" the poor? Gender, class and philanthropy in Victorian Britain', in G. Lewis (ed) *Forming Nation, Framing Welfare*, London: Routledge.

Mooney, G. and Fyfe, N. (2004) 'Active communities of resisting: contesting the Govanhill Pool closure in Glasgow, 2001-2002', Paper presented at the Social Policy Association Annual Conference, University of Nottingham, 13-15 July.

Moreland, M. (2007) *Mental Health Service User Movement?*, BBC Action Network (www.bbc.co.uk/dna/actionnetwork/A19232705).

Mullaly, B. (1997) *Structural Social Work: Ideology, Theory and Practice* (2nd edn), Oxford: Oxford University Press.

Muncie, J. (2004) *Youth and Crime* (2nd edn), London: Sage Publications.

Muncie, J. and Goldson, B. (2006) 'England and Wales: the new correctionalism', in J. Muncie and B. Goldson (eds) *Comparative Youth Justice*, London: Sage Publications.

Murray, C. (1990) *The Emerging British Underclass*, London: Institute of Economic Affairs.

Murray, C. (1994) *Underclass: The Crisis Deepens*, London: Institute of Economic Affairs.

Napo (National Association of Probation Officers) (2005) *Napo's Response to the Home Office Consultation Paper: 'Restructuring Probation to Reduce Re-Offending'*, London: Napo.

NCVO (National Council for Voluntary Organisations) (2007) *Involving Service Users: A Sound Strategy?*, Adventures in Strategy 2, London: NCVO/ The Performance Hub.

Neale, J. (2001) *The American War*, London: Bookmarks.

ONS (Office for National Statistics) (2004) *Focus on Social Inequalities*, London: The Stationery Office.

Oppenheim, C. (1997) 'The growth of poverty and inequality', in A. Walker and C. Walker (eds) *Britain Divided: The Growth of Social Exclusion in the 1980s and 1990s*, London: Child Poverty Action Group.

Orcutt, B. (1990) *Science and Inquiry in Social Work Practice*, New York, NY: Columbia University Press.

Orme, J. (2001) 'Regulation or fragmentation? Directions for social work under New Labour', *British Journal of Social Work*, 31 (4), 611-24.

Pantazis, C. and Ruspini, E. (2006) 'Gender, poverty and social exclusion', in C. Pantazis, D. Gordon and R. Levitas (eds) *Poverty and Social Exclusion in Britain: The Millennium Survey*, Bristol: The Policy Press.

Parton, N. and O'Byrne, P. (2000) *Constructive Social Work*, Basingstoke: Macmillan.

Paxton, W., Pearce, N., Unwin, J. and Molyneux, P. (2005) *The Voluntary Sector Delivering Public Services: Transfer or Transformation?*, York: Joseph Rowntree Foundation.

Payne, G. (ed) (2006) *Social Divisions* (2nd edn), Basingstoke: Palgrave.

Payne, M. (2002) 'The role and achievements of a professional association in the late twentieth century: the British Association of Social Workers 1970–2000', *British Journal of Social Work*, 32 (8), 969-95.

Payne, M. (2005) *The Origins of Social Work*, Basingstoke: Palgrave Macmillan.

Pearson, G. (1975) 'Making social workers: bad promises and good omens', in R. Bailey and M. Brake (eds) *Radical Social Work*, London: Edward Arnold.

Pease, B. and Fook, J. (eds) (1999a) *Transforming Social Work Practice: Postmodern Critical Perspectives*, London: Routledge.

Pease, B. and Fook, J. (1999b) 'Postmodern theory and emancipatory social work', in B. Pease and J. Fook (eds) *Transforming Social Work Practice: Postmodern Critical Perspectives*, London: Routledge.

Pedersen, S. (2004) *Eleanor Rathbone and the Politics of Conscience*, Yale, CT: Yale University Press.

Penketh, L. (2000) *Tackling Institutional Racism*, Bristol: The Policy Press.

Pithouse, A. and Crowley, A. (2007) 'Adults rule? Children, advocacy and complaints to social services', *Children and Society*, 21 (3), 201-13.

Pollock, A. (2004) *NHS plc: The Privatisation of our Health Care*, London: Verso.

Popay, J. and Dhooge, Y. (1989) 'Unemployment, cod's head soup and radical social work', in M. Langan and P. Lee (eds) *Radical Social Work Today*, London: Unwin Hyman.

Popple, K. (2006) 'Community development in the 21st century: a case of conditional development', *British Journal of Social Work*, 36 (2), 333-40.

Powell, F. (2001) *The Politics of Social Work*, London: Sage Publications.

Powell, F. and Geoghegan, M. (2005) 'Reclaiming civil society: the future of global social work?', *European Journal of Social Work*, 8 (2), 129-44.

Preston, G. (2005) 'Conclusion', in G. Preston (ed) *At Greatest Risk: The Children Most Likely to be Poor*, London: Child Poverty Action Group.

Preston-Shoot, M. (2004) 'Responding by degrees: surveying the education and practice landscape', *Social Work Education*, 23 (6), 667-92.

Preston-Shoot, M. (2007) *Effective Groupwork*, Basingstoke: Palgrave Macmillan.

Price, V. and Simpson, G. (2007) *Transforming Society? Social Work and Sociology*, Bristol: The Policy Press.

Prout, A., Tisdall, K., Hill, M. and Davies, J. (eds) (2006) *Children, Participation and Social Inclusion*, Bristol: The Policy Press.

Puigvert, L. and Elboj, C. (2004) 'Interactions among "other women": creating personal and social meaning', *Journal of Social Work Practice*, 18 (3), 351-64.

Quetelet, A. (1996 [1842]) 'Of the development of the propensity to crime', in J. Muncie, E. McLaughlin and M. Langan (eds) *Criminological Perspectives: A Reader*, London: Sage (as abridged from the original paper, 'A treatise on man', Edinburgh: Chambers).

Qureshi, R. (2007) 'Something remarkable: the arrival of asylum seekers in Glasgow's poorest areas has fostered a new community spirit', *The Guardian*, 13 April.

Ramsden, K. and Stevenson, J. (2006) *Asylum in Scotland: Children's Welfare Paramount? A Guide for Members of BASW and UNISON Scotland*, Glasgow: UNISON/BASW.

Rapley, J. (2004) *Globalization and Inequality*, London: Lynne Rienner Publishers.

Refugee Council (2001) *A Case for Change: How Refugee Children in England are Missing Out*, London: Refugee Council, in association with The Children's Society and Save the Children.

Reisch, M. and Andrews, J. (2002) *The Road Not Taken: A History of Radical Social Work in the United States*, New York, NY: Brunner-Routledge.

Revans, L. (2008) 'Newly qualified social workers: surviving the first year', *Community Care*, 28 February.

Richards, S., Hickman, G. and Aiers, A. (2008) 'Involving looked after young people in the design and delivery of the social work curriculum', Workshop held at the Joint Social Work Education Conference, Cambridge, 10 July (www.jswec.co.uk/presentations/W18%20Involving%20Looked%20After%20Children%20in%20the%20D&D%20of%20Curriculum.ppt).

Ritchie, A. and Woodward, R. (2009: forthcoming) '"Changing Lives": critical reflections on the social work change programme for Scotland', *Critical Social Policy*, in press.

Robinson, G. and Burnett, R. (2007) 'Experiencing modernization: frontline probation perspectives on the transition to a National Offender Management Service', *Probation Journal*, 54 (4), 31–8.

Rogers, A. and Pilgrim, D. (1991) 'Pulling down Churches: accounting for the British mental health users' movement', *Sociology of Health and Illness*, 13 (2), 129–48.

Rosenberg, J. (2000) *The Follies of Globalization*, London: Verso.

Rowbotham, S. (1975) *Hidden from History: 300 Years of Women's Oppression and the Fight Against It*, London: Pluto Press.

RWSG (Refugee Women's Strategy Group) (2007) *Our Voices Matter: A Summary Report of Issues and Recommendations from Refugee and Asylum Seeking Women Living in Glasgow*, Glasgow: RWSG/Scottish Refugee Council.

Sanders, V. (2001) 'First wave feminism', in S. Gamble (ed) *Feminism and Postfeminism*, London: Routledge.

Schorr, A. (1992) *The Personal Social Services: An Outside View*, York: Joseph Rowntree Foundation.

SCIE (Social Care Institute for Excellence) (2007) *Transferring Knowledge, Transforming Practice*, London: SCIE.

Scottish Executive (2000) *Report of the Joint Future Group*, Edinburgh: Scottish Executive.

Scottish Executive (2001a) *For Scotland's Children*, Edinburgh: Scottish Executive.

Scottish Executive (2001b) *Independent Advocacy: A Guide for Commissioners*, Edinburgh: Scottish Executive.

Scottish Executive (2003) *The Framework for Social Work Education in Scotland*, Edinburgh: Scottish Executive.

Scottish Executive (2005) *Getting It Right for Every Child: Proposals For Action, Section 3, Integrated Assessment, Planning and Recording Framework*, Edinburgh: Scottish Executive.

Scottish Executive (2006a) *Changing Lives: Report of the 21st Century Social Work Review*, Edinburgh: Scottish Executive.

Scottish Executive (2006b) *Key Capabilities in Child Care and Protection*, Edinburgh: Scottish Executive.

Scottish Government/COSLA (Convention of Scottish Local Authorities) (2007) *Concordat between the Scottish Government and Local Government*, Edinburgh: Scottish Government (www.scotland.gov.uk/Resource/Doc/923/0054147.pdf).

Scourfield, P. (2007) 'Social care and the modern citizen: client, consumer, service user, manager and entrepreneur', *British Journal of Social Work*, 37 (1), 107-22.

SCVO (Scottish Council for Voluntary Organisations) (2007) *Fair Funding for Voluntary Service Sector* (www.scvo.org.uk/scvo/PolicyAndParliament).

Seebohm Committee (1968) *Report of the Committee on Local Authority and Allied Social Services*, Cmnd 3703, London: HMSO.

Sergeant, J. (1998) 'UK politics: the major scandal sheet', *The Guardian*, 27 October.

Shardlow, S. (1989) *The Values of Change in Social Work*, London: Routledge.

Sharkey, P. (2000) 'Community work and community care: links in practice and education', *Social Work Education*, 19 (1), 7-17.

Simpkin, M. (1983) *Trapped Within Welfare?* (2nd edn), Basingstoke: Macmillan.

Singh, G. and Cowden, S. (2006) 'The social worker as intellectual: reclaiming a critical praxis', Paper presented at the Joint Social Work Education Conference, Cambridge University, 12-14 July (www.swapexternal.soton.ac.uk/jswec2006/jswec_presentations/room%20119/The%20Social%20Worker%20as%20Intellectual.ppt#1).

Skills for Care (2005) *The State of the Social Care Workforce 2004*, Leeds: Skills for Care.

Skinner, A. (2001) *Service Users' Views of Social Services Departments*, Research Note, Leicester: Centre for Social Action, De Montfort University.

Smith, D. (2004) 'The uses and abuses of positivism', in G. Mair (ed) *What Matters in Probation?*, Cullompton: Willan.

Spencer, S. (2006) *Migration and Integration: The Impact of NGOs on Future Policy Development in Ireland*, Oxford: Oxford University Centre on Migration, Policy and Society (compas) (www.compas.ox.ac.uk/publications/papers/Irish%20NGOs%20full%20report.pdf).

Stanley, K. (2001) *Cold Comfort: Young Separated Refugees in England*, London: Save the Children.

Stedman-Jones, G. (1984) *Outcast London* (2nd edn), Oxford: Clarendon Press.

Stepney, P. (2006) 'Mission impossible? Critical practice in social work', *British Journal of Social Work*, 36 (8), 1289-307.

Stevenson, O. (2005) 'Genericism and specialization: the story since 1970', *British Journal of Social Work*, 35 (5), 569-86.

Thompson, N. (2002) 'Social movements, social justice and social work', *British Journal of Social Work*, 32 (6), 711-22.

Thompson, N. (2006) *Anti-Discriminatory Practice* (4th edn), London: Palgrave Macmillan.

Thornham, S. (2001) 'Second wave feminism', in S. Gamble (ed) *Feminism and Postfeminism*, London: Routledge.

TOPSS (Training Organisation for the Personal Social Services) (2002) *The National Occupational Standards for Social Work*, Leeds: TOPSS (now Skills for Care).

Trevithick, P. (2005) *Social Work Skills: A Practice Handbook* (2nd edn), Maidenhead: Open University Press.

Tsui, M. and Cheung, F.C.H. (2004) 'Gone with the wind: the impacts of managerialism on human services', *British Journal of Social Work*, 34 (3), 437-42.

Twelvetrees, A. (2008 [1982]) *Community Work* (4th edn), Basingstoke: Macmillan.

UNICEF (United Nations Children's Fund) (2007) *Report Card 7, Child Poverty in Perspective: An Overview of Child Wellbeing in Rich Countries*, Florence, Italy: UNICEF Innocenti Research Centre (www.unicef-icdc. org/presscentre/presskit/reportcard7/rc7_eng.pdf).

Walters, R. and Woodward, R. (2007) 'Punishing poor parents: "respect", "responsibility" and parenting orders in Scotland', *Youth Justice*, 7 (1), 5-20.

Walton, R. (2005) 'Social work as a social institution', *British Journal of Social Work*, 35 (5), 587-607.

Webb, A. and Wistow, G. (1987) *Social Work, Social Care and Social Planning: The Personal Social Services since Seebohm*, London: Longman.

Webb, S. (2001) 'Some considerations on the validity of evidence-based practice in social work', *British Journal of Social Work*, 31 (1), 57-79.

Webb, S. (2003) 'Local orders and global chaos in social work', *European Journal of Social Work*, 6 (2), 191-204.

Wells, M. and Hoikkala, S. (2004) 'A comparison of two European resettlement programmes for young separated refugees', in D. Hayes and B. Humphries (eds) *Social Work, Immigration and Asylum*, London: Jessica Kingsley Publishers.

Whelan, R. (2001) *Helping the Poor: Friendly Visiting, Dole Charities and Dole Queues*, London: Civitas.

White, R. and Cunneen, C. (2006) 'Social class, youth crime and justice', in B. Goldson and J. Muncie (eds) *Youth Crime and Justice*, London: Sage Publications.

White, V. (2006) *The State of Feminist Social Work*, London: Routledge.

White, V. and Harris, J. (2007) 'Management', in M. Lymbery and K. Postle (eds) *Social Work: A Companion to Learning*, London: Sage Publications.

Whitmore, E. and Wilson, M.G. (2004) 'Popular resistance to global corporate rule: the role of social work (with a little help from Gramsci and Freire)', in I. Ferguson, M. Lavalette and E. Whitmore (eds) *Globalisation, Global Justice and Social Work*, London: Routledge.

Wilkinson, R. (2005) *The Impact of Inequality: How to Make Sick Societies Healthier*, New York, NY: The Free Press.

Williams, F. (1996) 'Postmodernism, feminism and the question of difference', in N. Parton (ed) *Social Theory, Social Change and Social Work*, London: Routledge.

Willis, M. (2007) 'Independence Day', *Community Care*, 8 March (www.communitycare.co.uk).

Wilson, K., Ruch, G., Lymbery, M. and Cooper, A. (2008) *Social Work: An Introduction to Contemporary Practice*, Harlow: Pearson Education.

Wolmar, C. (2000) *The Secret Abuse Scandal in Children's Homes*, London: Vision Paperbacks.

Woodward, R. (2006) 'I still have the right to be heard: looked after children and the participation agenda', Paper presented at the University of Stirling Seminar Series, Department of Applied Social Science, 25 January.

Woodward, R. (2007) *Young People's Experience of, and Participation in, the Fostering Process*, Interim Report, Paisley: Kibble Education and Care Services.

Woodward, R. and Mackay, K. (2008) 'Exploring the place of values in social work education', Paper presented at the Joint Social Work Education Conference, Cambridge, 9–11 July (www.jswec.co.uk/presentations/JSWEC%201%202008%20-%20values.ppt).

Index